GLIMPSES THROUGH THE FOREST

Memories of Gabon

By

Jason Gray

A PEACE CORPS WRITERS BOOK

A Peace Corps Writers Book.

An imprint of Peace Corps Worldwide.

Glimpses through the Forest: Memories of Gabon
Copyright © 2013 by Jason Gray
All rights reserved.

ISBN-13: 978-1-935925-30-9
ISBN-10: 193592530X
Library of Congress Control Number: 2013934691

First Peace Corps Writers Edition, March 2013
Cover photo: Elephant crossing river, Gabon, 2005, by Jason Gray
All photos and images by Jason Gray unless otherwise indicated.

For my family,
with a special dedication to Linda,
and in loving memory of
Diamond Jim, O.G., and Harriet

Contents

Maps

EQUATORIAL
GUINEA

REPUBLIC OF
CONGO

GABON

Libreville

Equator

Port Gentil
Lambaréné

Iboundji
Koulamoutou

Setté
Cama

Gamba
Tchibanga

REPUBLIC OF
CONGO

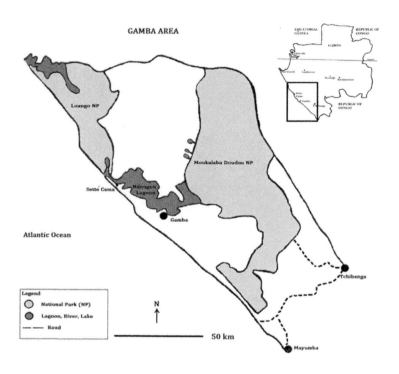

GAMBA AREA

Loango NP

Moukalaba Doudou NP

Setté Cama

Ndougou Lagoon

Gamba

Atlantic Ocean

Tchibanga

Mayumba

Legend

○ National Park (NP)

● Lagoon, River, Lake

- - - Road

N

50 km

Preface

If I close my eyes, sometimes, I can still draw in the smell, wafting on the salty breeze off of the middle Atlantic, pulling along hints of white sands and swaying palms...Gabon. This aroma awakens memories of life along the water, the forest, and the people of the Ndougou Lagoon. Filling my senses, that pungent, bittersweet combination of wet leaves and sea water reminds me of the glimpses of life seen through the forest, and pulls me back in my dreams and spirit to the heart of Africa, to where a piece of my heart still lingers.

Several years ago, I had the privilege of serving as a Peace Corps volunteer in the town of Gamba, in the Central African country of Gabon. A coastal nation, nearly 85 percent of which is covered by thick, tropical rain forest, Gabon is a remarkably diverse, vibrant, and mysterious place. Its people share a rich history and culture.

My assignment with the Peace Corps was to assist in the development of and training for a national environmental education program. At the end of my two-year service, I stayed to work with the Worldwide Fund for Nature (WWF). Much of this work is being continued by my friends and colleagues in Gabon, both by local Gabonese and by other conservationists. This collection of memories is not meant to highlight any individual project or assignment but rather to provide readers with a few glimpses into a place that many have not yet heard of.

After all these years away from Gabon, my memories are sometimes clear, sometimes hazy. They come back to me in flashes of colors and sounds, smells and emotion. I can still see a classroom of students, hands raised to answer a question. The strong scent left by an elephant disappearing into the trees remains imprinted on my mind.

What follows in the turning of these pages reflects these remembrances. While the memories are not presented in any chronological order, they do blend across the four seasons of Gabon, from the *grande saison sèche* (long dry season, lasting from May to September) to the *grande saison de pluie* (long rainy season, from September to December), followed by the *petite saison sèche* (short dry season, from December to February) and the *petite saison de pluie* (short rainy season, from February to May). As with any memoir, mistakes are my own. I hope merely to provide a setting to help explain these very personal recollections and to share with you my impressions of a remarkable place, its people, and its beauty.

May these stories transport you, as my experiences transported me.

Diboti.

—Jason Gray, 2013

Introduction to My Peace Corps Post

The airplane touched down as the sun rose, juxtaposing the dark skies through which we had made our descent with the emerging rosy orange of dawn. I remember a haze setting over the vague surroundings, making it hard to see exactly where it was that we had landed. The plane taxied to a stop, and as I followed the other passengers out and down the boarding stairs, I was struck by the weight of moisture in the still morning air, already pregnant with heat and dripping with humidity. I had arrived; we had arrived.

This was the first, as I saw it, official day of my Peace Corps service. I had joined a group of more than forty other volunteers-in-training in Philadelphia for a couple of days of medical examinations and shots, safety training, and ice-breaker exercises. And on June 29, 2002, after traveling from my home town in Montana to Philadelphia, taking a bus to

New York, and boarding a plane bound for Paris, France, then Africa, here we were, in Gabon.

The excitement, nervousness, and jet lag made me giddy. From the airport, after making our way through customs and meeting with our Peace Corps trainers and staff, we proceeded to a hotel-like dormitory for some additional talks on health conditions and a summary of what the next several months of training would entail. In all, the Peace Corps put us through three months of language, culture, and technical skills training, which included the most important training of all—living with a host family for the entire three months. Our training took place in Lambaréné, a town on the banks of the Ogooué River, made famous by Dr. Albert Schweitzer, and described in more detail in the main portions of this writing.

When I had received my Peace Corps assignment, I was initially classified as an agroforestry agent. While not fully sure what this would mean, I assumed it had to do with planting and growing trees. However, once I arrived in Gabon, along with other agroforestry agents, health volunteers, and English teachers, we were informed by Peace Corps Gabon administration that there was no Peace Corps agroforestry program in Gabon and that we would actually be working as environmental education agents. My fellow environmental education volunteers and I took this change of direction in stride as we commenced our training.

An environmental education agent's principal role was to work with primary school teachers, students, and administrators to integrate environmental education into their curricula. Our training helped us become comfortable designing short lesson plans, develop interesting and educational games, paint some simple wall murals of local flora and fauna for the students, and get our feet wet in an actual Gabonese school. Other than that, however, we were really on our own to figure out how best to try to implement our work, according to the local needs, conditions, resources, and interests of the communities in which we were being sent to live. This trial-and-error experimentation process was both a major excitement and frustration of Peace Corps service.

Our job was to assist in the development of and training for a national environmental education program and to train teachers to guide their students through the program. Shortly after our arrival in Gabon, the late, long-serving Gabonese president, El Hadj Omar Bongo Ondimba, had set aside eleven percent of the country in a system of thirteen national parks. It seemed he was determined to turn his country into an ecotourism hot spot, and the Peace Corps environmental education program was designed in part to help educate schoolchildren about the existence of these parks, the benefits of having them set aside as protected areas, and the importance of the resources within to the national economy. This goal, accompanied by the fact that many of the people living in and around the new national parks had no idea the lands they lived in were now national tourism and conservation priorities, promised to make the education aspect of our assignment quite interesting.

In addition to helping design teacher trainings, environmental education volunteers were encouraged to partner with local, national, and international environmental nonprofit organizations, school groups, and really anyone who could assist in integrating the volunteer into the community and help ensure the local school children were kept up to speed with the still-emerging national environmental education agenda.

At the close of our training in Lambaréné, we were scattered throughout the country, spread from the coast to the far eastern border with the Republic of Congo.

I was sent to the southwestern, near-coastal town of Gamba, in the Ogooué-Maritime Province. At the time (2002), Gamba had a population of roughly 7,000 people, and it is still home to an incredible diversity of wildlife, ecosystems, and colorful characters. It also hosts the dwindling stocks of onshore oil supplies, which for decades have topped off the country's coffers. As the center of operations for the Gabonese branch of the Shell Oil Company, Gamba is home to people from all over the world. A nearby expatriate community houses the European and African managers of Shell Gabon. In one day, in addition to encountering people from the local, indigenous villages, one could meet Gabonese from every part of the country, as well as Nigerians, Equatorial Guineans, French, Dutch, English, Scots, Nigeriens, Spanish, Cameroonian, Congolese, Ghanaians, Central Africans, Chinese, Japanese, Germans, Malaysians, Lebanese, Senegalese, Malians, Belgians, Moroccans, Togolese, Beninese—and me, the local Peace Corps volunteer.

With all of this diversity, it is easy to get lost in the nationalities and different cultures. For me, however, the blend of people and languages enriched this tiny metropolis. It also facilitated my work of bringing people of diverse backgrounds (ethnically and professionally) together to improve the local teachers' and students' understanding of the environmental challenges faced by the region.

In Gamba, I was fortunate in the amount of resources and people willing to work with me, both in the schools and on other projects. All volunteers are assigned a local counterpart with whom the volunteer works for most of his or her service. My counterpart, who became a near brother to me, was Jean Pierre Bayet, the founder of Ibonga, a local environmental nonprofit organization (www.ibonga.org). I spent most of my three years in Gabon partnering with Ibonga, which has become a mainstay in the local schools and the two national parks in the region—Loango National Park and Moukalaba-Doudou National Park.

Working through Ibonga, which was already active in such extracurricular activities in the schools as conducting trash cleanups, field trips for older students, and organizing celebrations for World Environment Day (June 5), I was given authorization from the regional school superintendent to work in all six primary schools of Gamba, and eventually, surrounding villages and towns. Jean Pierre and I developed and implemented a conservation-based curriculum, which we taught in fourth and fifth-grade level classes in Gamba, as well as in the villages of Setté Cama, Ibouka, and Mayonami. We brought in conservation workers, government officials, fishermen, and local and visiting international scientists to speak with the students. I helped Ibonga recruit the principals of the elementary schools to organize as the nonprofit's board of directors, and I also helped them raise funds through grants from embassies and foundations to purchase cleanup equipment, supplies for field trips, and, eventually, to conduct teacher trainings.

After we had taught our classes for close to two years and gotten the teachers and over six hundred students used to (and excited about) learning about the natural history of their region and the conservation efforts going on around them, Jean Pierre and I, along with some of my Peace Corps colleagues, helped Ibonga conduct several teacher trainings, involving approximately 80 teachers from two provinces.

Through our work in the schools, we were also able to participate in projects with the Smithsonian Institution, which was conducting biodiversity assessments in the region. Many times we were able to bring students along on these projects. The local researchers would come into the classrooms and talk about what they were doing, then we would bring students to the Smithsonian laboratory or go on field excursions. We also brought students out to visit a marine turtle research camp hosted by Ibonga, the Worldwide Fund for Nature (the international counterpart of the World Wildlife Fund in the United States) (WWF), and Protomac, a European Union–funded turtle research organization.

For all of this education and conservation work, the most important component was the fact that everyone agreed to funnel their efforts through Ibonga, the small, locally founded and locally run organization. This meant that the activities were done in a culturally appropriate, locally focused manner, by people who grew up in the region. The presence of foreign researchers and government officials from the capital, European conservation workers, and an American Peace Corps volunteer was merely a coup for the local nonprofit, not the driving force of its successes.

At the end of my two-year Peace Corps service, I was hired by WWF to continue building local capacity with Ibonga and with a fishermen's cooperative, and to further assist in the development of the environmental education curriculum.

For any prospective future Peace Corps Volunteers who might be reading this, I do feel that it is important to acknowledge that for all the excitement and frustrations of the actual work assignment, there are countless days and nights spent getting to know one's neighbors, community, and new friends. Some of those days and nights were quite difficult for me, and like any place, Gamba posed many challenges and some disappointments. It was a small town, with a certain degree of monotony and loneliness at first. Many nights were spent reading a book, listening to music, or watching my neighbors' children play in the sandy courtyard outside my house. Some days were so incredibly thick with heat and humidity that any work at all seemed impossible. And some lonely nights were spent remembering friends and family back home.

Although I do remember some not-so-exciting nights, a weekend or two suffering through malarial fevers, and various failed projects or frustrating relationships, my most precious memories convey for me a strong sense of the time and place in which I lived in Gamba and in Gabon. And although my experiences may not imbue me with any special wisdom or insight, for anyone contemplating joining the Peace Corps or attempting to work on international conservation or development work, I make the following recommendation: approach your decision with an open heart and mind, balanced expectations, and surrounded by whatever excitement you first had when you heard about the opportunity. For me, joining the Peace Corps was an opportunity to engage with the world in a way I had never done before; and living and working abroad, listening to others and learning from their viewpoints, and sharing my own, has helped me stay connected with the global community.

With this introductory background for why I was in Gabon, my goal with this book is to try to describe as vividly as I can the place as I experienced it, through stories and memories of my time with the Peace Corps and WWF. I am striving to convey the sights and sounds, the culture, food, language, and life that I experienced, partly to help me remember, but mostly to honor the people I met and the place I love.

In case these glimpses through the forest inspire you to learn more about Gabon, Gamba, and the conservation work underway in Central Africa, you will find a list of additional reading at the end of this book and in the occasional reference. For now, turn the page and prepare to enter the forest...

Part I: Discovering Gabon

Congratulations on your invitation to serve for 2 years
as a Peace Corps Volunteer in Gabon!...Your work in
Gabon will be challenging....Keep your expectations low
and your hopes high! At the end of it all, you will de-
part Gabon with more than you can ever hope to leave
behind.

—A WELCOME LETTER,
THE PEACE CORPS WELCOMES YOU TO GABON
(A PEACE CORPS PUBLICATION FOR NEW
VOLUNTEERS, MARCH 2002)

Mist on the Lagoon

⌘

The first thing you notice when arriving in Gamba, whether by plane or land, is the immensity of the forest. From the air, the forest seems to stretch out forever, a sea of greens and yellows, dotted with flashes of orange and red, that starts from clean, white beaches and leads the eye east into the depths of the Congo Basin. By land, the canopy high above appears like a cathedral ceiling, keeping you grounded, surrounded, and small. Thick trunks and branches and twisted vines blur as you drive along the impermanent-seeming road, a tapestry of verdant life.

The second thing you notice is the water. Most specifically, the Ndougou Lagoon. From the air, it suddenly sparkles out of the forest, stretching out fingers of reflective silver, dotted with hundreds of dark, forested islands, sprinkled here and there with long, dugout pirogues. By land, the forest gives way to small, coastal savannahs, from which a shimmering liquid vision may be glimpsed through the trees. The waters of the lagoon are fed from the surrounding forest, as rain soaks through the leaves and roots, rushes over the soil, and pours into the lagoon, full of dark reds and greens from the tannins in the leaves and the silt in the soil.

Early in the morning, water vapor hangs low and dense, waiting for the temperature to rise, then dissipates. This clinging mist is alive, whispering with the muted sounds of a tropical awakening. Bird calls seem disjointed as sound is reflected and deflected off invisible islands and dark waters. A fisherman setting off for an early start needs to shout to be heard by friends on the shore as the shroud sits heavy on the water. Even the buzzing roars from small outboard motors are drowned by the cloudy air.

These mists veil the true nature of the lagoon, the islands, and the forest. They create a sense of mysterious longing to see what hides within. From the bow of a pirogue, it is easy to imagine a monstrous beast rising up from the lagoon, unseen until it is upon you; or that an island that was not there the day before might suddenly block the way. And yet, the mists themselves may be the very essence of Gamba— mystery and adventure, yet an everyday occurrence. The name Gamba is thought to derive from the word for "fog" in Civili, one of the languages of the Ndougou Lagoon. Whether true or not, it fits. A skilled piroguier (a dugout boat pilot) like my counterpart, Jean Pierre Bayet, can navigate through the mist as if it was not there, having traveled the same route hundreds, perhaps thousands, of times through rain and sun, day and night.

On many a misty morning, I would tag along as a skilled passenger (meaning I would sit still and add ballast to the pirogue) as a group of friends set out to Setté Cama, one of several villages on the lagoon—and Jean Pierre's birthplace. The air was infused with moisture, and visibility was limited to about ten feet on all sides. Jean Pierre and I would talk in hushed voices upon leaving the sandy shores of Gamba town but would fall into deep, near reverent silence as every breath drank in the fog. This was a surreal sensation for me, with the pirogue seeming to float through a cloud rather than on the water, light, free, directionless. Shapes of islands and tall trees popped up at the outermost edge of my vision, yet it was impossible to know whether they were truly there. Then, slowly at first, the gray water became visible all around, as the mists began to rise. The veil lifted, burned away by the morning sun and soon-to-arrive heat. And the curtain of moisture parted, drawn aside, so that the previously imagined islands would appear for real.

Jean Pierre Bayet fishing with youth from Setté Cama

This was my favorite time of day on the lagoon, with a panoply of sights and a symphony of sounds piercing through the fading mist and coming full force on my senses. All of this life, the colors and smells and songs of the forest, was always there, waiting for the signal to come alive and start the day anew. At that exact moment, the pirogue ceased to float and seemed to sink down, to glide heavier on the water, more present, more real. Hornbills would fly by overhead, flapping their heavy wings to rise up and out, then pulling the wings in as their weighted bills seemed to drag them down to earth, a laborious, jerky flight. And in the trees, flocks of African Grey Parrots would call out, scratchy-throated and loud, rejoicing in the now-clear air, as the last tendrils of mist were absorbed into the trees. The parrots' bright red tails stood out vividly against the morning light and the backdrop of emerald leaves. The old outboard motor picked up in decibels, but not enough to drown out the other sounds. And we would slowly start to talk again, to laugh at some joke or at my pronunciation of a phrase in Yilumbu (another language of the Ndougou). Jean Pierre would point out the powerful fish eagles circling overhead and a jumping flash of silver in the water as a school of barracuda flushed out their prey. The curtain had lifted, the day come again.

For me, the morning mist was like a prelude, covering over a magnificent masterpiece, unveiled in the instant when patience starts to run thin and anticipation runs thick. And I remember that feeling, like the cresting of a steep hill with a beautiful vista laid out before me, the feel of sitting in the boat, waiting for the mists to lift to show the wonder beyond.

And then we would arrive in Setté Cama—or wherever we happened to be going—where, after a long day of work or play, we would surrender to a well-earned sleep and awaken to another misty morning. Even after all this time away from Gabon, I still sometimes fall asleep, dreaming of the mist on the lagoon, eager for the uncovering of the mysteries beyond.

Forest Elephants in the Grass

@⁓@

The first time I saw them, I was pedaling along on my Peace Corps–issued bicycle, weaving around hard-packed potholes where the pavement met red, dusty laterite. The savannah grass reached up five feet tall, seeded flower-heads drooping like heavy archways, each one leading into another. The grass sprouted out of the hard, clayish soils mixed with sand, lying dormant under the earth until the rains came, then rushing up in frantic competition to be the first to reach out and embrace the sun.

A car stopped beside me, and a woman leaned out, pointing toward the forest edge. I stopped, asking her what I was looking for. She smiled and merely kept pointing, as if to say, "you have so much still to learn." Then she said, "There...," directing my eyes to the west, toward the forest. I had to strain to see over the grass, peering into the slowly fading day as early afternoon clouds began to hide the sun. I thought, *I'd better keep going, or I'll be biking back in the dark.* Then, suddenly, I saw them. Movement blurred the edge of the small strip of coastal forest. One, two, three. Three gray-skinned ghosts stepped lightly into the grass, edging along the tree line in single file. They were bulky, somehow squat and huge at the same time. Swishing tails and hanging trunks, they seemed to be playing follow-the-leader. Elephants. My first forest elephants.

I caught my breath, a wide grin slowly growing on my dusty face. I couldn't look away; I couldn't believe my eyes. I had seen elephants before in Kenya—big savannah giants, bathing and carousing with their family members, as is their wont. However, these shy creatures now reentering the forest were different. Smaller in stature, smaller in tusk, elusive, and forest-dwelling. These were forest elephants. Laughing, I turned to thank the woman in the car. She smiled and said "Welcome to Gamba." With that, she drove off down the road. I remained motionless for a few more minutes, gazing into the forest, hoping to catch another glimpse of these magnificent creatures.

Over the next several years, I was to come into contact with elephants quite frequently. I remember another instance in which I came much closer to an elephant while riding my bike. I had been in Gamba for several months and was beginning to get to know the lay of the land—back roads I could take to get to the Terminal (Shell's offices and pipeline terminal) to check my e-mail or conduct the necessary, if annoying, task of going to the only bank in the region, and quicker routes around town or to the beach. On this day, I was heading to check my e-mail (a weekly routine), and I decided to take a more direct pipeline road rather than follow the main paved road. These roads are seldom traveled by human traffic, aside from the occasional oil worker checking on the oil wells and pipelines connecting them to the Terminal. The roads make excellent sites to view birds and other wildlife, as they offer rare openings into the otherwise closed forest.

On this instance, I was enjoying the still air and listening for monkeys. I had seen several mustached monkeys a week before and could now hear a troop in the distance. I paused for ten minutes or so, absorbing the sounds of the insects I could not see and the occasional *whoosh-whirr* of liquids and gas rushing through the adjacent red pipes. Failing to spot the noisy but receding primates, I hopped back on my bike and continued on my route. I was not really in a hurry but was nonetheless proceeding at a brisk clip.

Ahead of me, I spotted an open metal gateway, which I assumed could be used to block the road to traffic when maintenance or other activities were being conducted. The gateway had an overhead crossbar, red like the pipelines. The road ran through the gateway and curved around a slight bend, with tall bushes on either side. As I approached the bend, I heard a soft sound coming from around it, roughly fifteen feet in front of me. I touched my brakes to slow down at the same time as a lumbering elephant, covered in dust, rounded the bend. We each stopped short, me with a skid of my tires and the elephant with a wide-eyed snort.

Thoughts flashed through my mind, judging the distance between us, the surrounding bushes and trees, the gateway. With roughly ten feet of empty road separating me from the elephant, I really did not have time to process any of these thoughts. Instead, I quickly backed away until I was behind the vertical red bar of the gateway. I kept my bike between me and the road and fervently hoped that this startled creature would not decide to test the strength of the metal bar. The elephant's eyes remained wide, keeping me directly in its line of sight. Those eyes seemed to drink me in, assessing my worth and whether or not I was a threat. If I had been more possessed of my nerves, I would have probably been able to determine the creature's gender. However, I was somewhat (or greatly) shaken, and I am now relegated to calling it an "it." The elephant must have seen through my adopted posture of nonthreatening calm (or more likely assessed my frozen fear) and decided I did not pose a serious threat to it. Slowly swinging its massive head, it turned from the road and walked quietly into the bushes and the forest.

I strained for several minutes to hear how far away it had gone, but I lost sight and sound of it almost immediately. Only the still-lingering smell of musk remained to prove the elephant had ever been there. The speed and softness with which these amazing beings move has never ceased to astound me. By contrast, my beating heart pounded in my ears, and the adrenaline coursing through my veins took much more time to dissipate, leaving me drained but amazed at this close encounter. I breathed in a final time, memorizing the pungent pachydermal perfume, hopped back on my bike, and continued on toward the Terminal.

Forest elephants in Loango National Park

What makes forest elephants so fascinating? First of all, they live in the forest. Although they are much smaller, on average, than their savannah cousins, these animals are still enormous. Imagine how difficult it can be to walk through the forest—any forest really, but especially a lush, tropical rainforest, with its clinging vines and frequent tight spaces. Now imagine trying to walk through that same forest without making a sound, while, at the same time, enjoying a height of eight feet and a weight of between one and three tons.

In addition, forest elephants (*Loxodonta cyclotis*) were recently distinguished (genetically) as a separate species from the larger savannah elephants (*Loxodonta africana*).[1] They live in herds like their cousins, but the herds are a great deal smaller, due to the amount of space they must share with trees. Much study has been (and continues to be) conducted on the vocalizations of elephants in general, and forest elephants in particular.[2] It is estimated that an infrasonic rumble from a forest elephant may allow it to communicate up to four kilometers away in the forest.[3]

Disturbingly, poaching of forest elephants from the Congo Basin appears to be on the rise, and illicit ivory trade continues to threaten all elephants.[4] While more research will surely go into understanding and protecting these beautiful beings, what is already clear is that the forests of Central Africa would not be the same without the forest elephants, just like my memories of those forests would not be the same without my memories of the elephants.

Bathing in the Ndougou

It's funny, the sense of cleanliness one feels after taking a bath, washing with soap, or sometimes even just washing with water. And the water, whether from a shower, a faucet, or a bucket, can rejuvenate the spirit, cleaning away grime both physical and mental. A bucket bath is simply what it sounds like—water in a bucket with which to wash. In Gabon, many people take bucket baths, heading to a communal pump or well to fill a large bucket (usually a plastic one) with water, and then using a cup to pour water over the head and body, then lathering up with hard, unscented soap, and rinsing with the same bucket-to-cup-to-body water transfer. This activity becomes second nature and is preferably conducted out of sight of others.

A bucket bath is a great way to conserve water, although the primary reason it is such a prevalent method of cleansing is the lack of indoor plumbing. Tepid water from a well or pump is a good way to cool off after a hot day, without the risk of being too cold. For those in need either of heat or the reassurance that the water itself is clean, boiling the water first is a good option.

Bucket bath by Erick Guerra
(Gabon Peace Corps Volunteer 2002-2004)

As much as I love a good bucket bath, though, there are other manners of cleansing that are equally good. One I do not advocate, but which certain people seem to enjoy, is taking a quick dip in the ocean. Salt water is great for wounds and external parasites, but the salt itself always leaves me feeling sticky and itchy. Another way to clean off sweat and ticks is to roll around in the dirt or mud. However, this type of "bath" seems more prevalent with elephants and buffalo than with humans. Yet another way of "cleansing" oneself is the proverbial "shower in a can," which involves using smelly deodorant to simply mask one's actual odor. This is a useful method of last resort after, for instance, a long day (or week) of hiking in the forest, before a dinner appointment at the local grilled fish restaurant without the necessary time to stop off at home to wash.

In villages on the rivers of Gabon, one can wash in the river, assuming the current is not too strong. This type of bath is brisk and often chilly, but also free for those who live nearby. A similar bathing technique is probably my favorite method in Gabon: bathing in the Ndougou Lagoon.

The lagoon has various zones, depending on how close one is to the ocean. Close to the mouth of the lagoon, where the sea waters come in, the water is murky from silt and sand, and quite salty. As the tides push inland, freshwater draining into the lagoon from the forest dilutes the salt. Near Setté Cama village, the salt is noticeable, but not by much. Further in, the water remains brackish, until it gradually loses all salinity by the time it reaches Gamba town. The mangrove forests on the edge of the lagoon also extend only as far as the brackish waters. Once the salinity is gone, so are the mangroves.

My favorite place to bathe in the Ndougou is at Setté Cama. The waters near the village have a slow, fairly strong current, due to the tides, but are manageable even by the children. Most villagers grew up with those waters, and a frequent sight in Setté Cama is children (and adults) splashing and playing in the water. The bravest swimmers would swim across the lagoon to the far side to check their manioc plantations hidden by mangroves on the lagoon banks, a swim of roughly one hundred yards. Although this might not seem that far, the muddy waters can hide logs, crocodiles, and other unseen obstacles.

I liked to bathe early in the morning, when the forest world awakened. Pied kingfishers would cry their shrill song, hovering over the water like miniature feathered kites, then dive in to snatch at fish. Small fish jumped as larger fish gave chase. The occasional hoot and laugh of a chimpanzee across the water would bounce off the trees and echo across the lagoon. And the fishermen would already be loaded up with their nets, heading out to their favorite fishing holes. And I would stand chest deep in the not-too-cold water, watching all of this life unfurl around me.

I remember strolling through the village, watching the children splash, young mothers bathing their infants, and old men standing in the water as they splashed water onto and into their pirogues to keep them wet and clean. One afternoon, as I walked through the village along the shore on my way to visit Jean Pierre at his house, I surprised a young woman roughly the same age as me, the niece of one of my colleagues, bathing. Embarrassed, I started to turn away. She called out, laughing, and unabashedly stood up, dripping water everywhere, beautiful, glistening, clean. Seeing me blush, she laughed harder and motioned for me to come closer, to talk or join in the bathing. I politely declined and fled, her laughter chasing me along my way.

And this water, this liquid highway for boats and animals, blended in with the surrounding trees. It was lovely.

My most memorable bathing story occurred one evening when I decided to take a quick swim and wash up for dinner. I do not remember who I was eating with, or what we ate, but I'll never forget my bath. I finished my swim and stood not ten feet from shore, in water up to my stomach. I had soap in my hand and was washing my arms and hair. Once I was good and lathered, I would sink down under the water to rinse off, as small hermit crabs crawled over my feet. I sank down, shaking my head under water to get the soap off, and surfaced for air. As my head rose from the water, I heard a loud snort and felt a spray of water from behind me. I froze, as seconds seemed to stretch into hours, knowing that only one thing could make such a sound—like a horse blowing out its breath after taking a deep drink from a mountain stream. My eyes widened, taking in the fading light reflected off the lagoon. Visions flashed through my mind as I struggled to remain calm, all the while aware of the potential danger in which I found myself.

Slowly, trying not to make any noise or rapid movements, I turned around and came face to face with what I feared was there. Large, liquid-black eyes gazed at me from in between two rounded ears, and enormous nostrils flared slightly, taking in my scent. There, not five feet from where I stood, was a hippopotamus, staring curiously straight at me.

Hippos can be extremely dangerous; they are thought to account for more fatalities among humans than any other large mammal in all of Africa. They can be deadly on land—and more so in their aquatic environment. Many a pirogue has been capsized by these extremely territorial creatures. So, with my heart in my throat, and likely sweating away all my recent cleanliness, I fled once more, straight out of the water and up the sloped shore to the house where I was staying. This time, I only imagined the laughter chasing me. I turned around, once I'd reached the porch of the house, and sat down to watch what the hippo would do. It simply watched me, then disappeared underwater to reappear a few minutes later, fifty feet out from the shore, and eventually disappeared altogether.

Frequently, two young hippos could be seen in that very spot, playing leap frog (or really, leap hippo), and I came to suspect that this was one of those youngsters, looking for someone to play with.

Road to Tchibanga

When I learned I would be assigned to live in Gabon, one of the first things I did was buy a detailed map of the country. Where was this place, what did it look like two-dimensionally, what geographic features did it have, where did its people live? And on that map, purchased at a map store in Pioneer Square in Portland, Oregon, I noticed several interesting things.

First, there was a lot of forest in Gabon. Green, light and dark and deep, stretched nearly from the coast all the way to the border of the Republic of Congo. And interspersed within that green were elevation markers of several mountain ranges, deep blue rivers, and the occasional savannahs along the coast and on the eastern side of the country, in the Plateau Batéké. The tallest mountain, Mount Iboundji, rose to 1,500 meters.

Second, there were not very many towns in much of the country. Most of the population (nearly half) lived in the capital, Libreville. Other large population centers were Port Gentil on the central coast, Lambaréné and Tchibanga in the central and southern interior, and Franceville near the Plateau Batéké.

Third, the legend showed several different types of roads, from permanent highway to intermittent, unpaved roads, to seasonal roads. Growing up in Montana, I was used to traveling unpaved roads—and even a few seasonal roads, in places with heavy snow pack. But one of the roads on this map stated that it was only open for about six months out of the year. This road ran through a yellow stretch of coastal savannah that wound its way west and north of the Nyanga River to the town of Gamba.

Months later, I came to truly understand the nature of that "seasonal" road. Early one day, I crowded into a pickup truck in the town center. Demsey, a friend of mine who worked for a European Union ecotourism project, was driving. Like most drivers in Gamba, Demsey had the necessary combination of sheer confidence in his own skills as a wheelman and utter crazy daring to tackle anything in his path. He had even given himself the nickname of "*Mujahedeen*," in a well-intentioned, albeit poor, attempt at humor and to try to convey his audacious sense of self-worth. I mention this as a testament to what is needed to embark on this road as a driver.

This was the dry season, and we were headed to the neighboring province, to the town of Tchibanga. From Gamba town, we traveled for about forty-five minutes on a tightly-packed, well-maintained laterite road to Mayonami, a small fishing town and port on the Nyanga River. From there, up to two vehicles at a time load onto a metal barge, powered at various times by one or two outboard motors, which then winds along the river, depositing its cargo and passengers further downstream. Once past this point, we entered the Plaine Ouanga (Ouanga Plains).

The Ouanga Plains are a narrow patch of savannah nestled between an equally narrow patch of coastal forest and the thicker forest that stretches out to the east. The ground is composed of fine sand particles, from which seasonal grasses grow tall and thick. The dry season fluffs out the sand so that only an experienced driver will have any luck making it through, as a pickup or Land Cruiser must weave and bob, zig and zag, to avoid becoming encumbered in the sand. The term *road* is not quite appropriate at any time of year, anywhere on the Ouanga Plains, as the path is really only that which a vehicle tries to make, passing over the sand with enough velocity to try to keep from becoming stuck.

Traversing the Ouanga Plains is quite a rodeo in the dry season. Passengers are thrown around like sacks of rice, as seatbelts are either nonexistent or insufficient, given the number of passengers in a vehicle.

This dry season is the "six months in which travel is possible," according to my old map from Portland. Once the rains come, the road becomes a completely different sort of beast. At the height of the rainy season, the sandy savannah becomes a shallow lake, with four to five feet of water throughout, enough to support a healthy population of fish and ample mud. Once this "impassable" road hazard forms, a driver's true skills are tested.

Most vehicles that pass over this route have large snorkels attached, so that water entering into the engine block does not get into the air intake valve. This essential feature is especially needed in those frequent instances where the road dips deep in the mud and the reddish waters reach up and over the hood of the vehicle, sometimes coming up onto the windshield. On one trip I was sitting in the front passenger seat, looking out the closed window as water reached about a foot up the window, nearly even with my head.

The trick to this road, whether in the wet or dry season, is timing. To avoid getting stuck, the vehicle needs to have enough acceleration to bounce over the sand or hit the water with enough force to carry it through the deepest spots. But no matter how good a driver is or claims to be, getting stuck is usually inevitable. The only hope is that the passengers are able to push it through the sand or back it out of the water, so the driver can get a good running start and pass beyond.

On this particular occasion, with Demsey at the wheel, we were flying across the sand, making good time, about halfway through the savannah. Demsey the *Mujahedeen*, the warrior-driver of the Ouanga Plains, slowed for a moment, gauging which existing rut to follow, when it happened. The truck lurched to a halt, jumbling us around in the cab and the bed. Stuck. We all got out and pushed and pulled, placing wooden planks kept in the truck bed for this very reason under the tires, until we got back on more solid ground. But the vehicle would not go more than a few feet before getting stuck again. Eventually, Demsey crawled under the truck and popped his head out, smirking. One of the metal struts was broken. With his usual aplomb, he grabbed a machete from behind the seat, trotted off into the woods, and returned a short time later with several large branches. He strapped these branches over the broken strut with twine, and placed a couple more branches in the back of the truck. Off we went, stopping once more to replace the now broken branches.

Finally, the road lead through a short patch of forest to another bend in the river called Boumé Boumé, at which point a single-vehicle, hand-pulled ferry barge sat. A bridge was, and probably still is, being constructed over this narrow branch of the river, but during my time, it was of no use.[5]

After Boumé Boumé, the road hardens, turning to clay as it heads inland, away from the coast. In the rainy season, this clay is thick, gooey mud, through which a vehicle may slide and skitter, rolling over or skidding off a steep hill. In the dry season, the marks left by previous vehicles during the muddy season leave deep crevasses in the road. Again, the trick is timing, skill, and luck.

Drivers need to know how their vehicles skid and turn; they need to feel the road through the steering wheel. Over the crevasses, eroded by the departed rains, a driver needs to feel how far he or she can tip one side of the vehicle so that the wheels do not get stuck in one rut, while not tipping over. This ends up rendering a fairly short trip (distancewise) into an ordeal of hours, painstakingly turning this way and that, braking over one patch only to accelerate over the next. Finally, first laterite, then pavement appears, and one can cruise into the provincial capital of Tchibanga.

With Demsey as both driver and makeshift auto repairman, fixing the strut with branches, we somehow got all the way to Tchibanga, where a professional mechanic fitted the truck with an actual, metal replacement strut before our return trip. This road, over sand, through four-foot-deep water and sand traps, and over two ferries, is the national highway connecting Gamba to the rest of the country.

This road, this adventure, this "seasonal" route, is the path over which much of the commercial goods bought and sold in Gamba must travel. True, they can come up the Nyanga River via barge to Mayonami, and via airplane at the Gamba Airport, but most people, food items, and goods travel along the road from Tchibanga. If the route were paved, with a few working bridges in between, it would take roughly one hour. The fastest I have ever done it was in over four hours. The slowest was nearly twelve, but I still considered that to be lucky, as many other travelers have been stranded completely with their vehicle stuck or broken down. The risks one takes on the road to Tchibanga!

Bush taxi stuck in the Ouanga Plains on the road to Tchibanga

Taxi-Brousse

T he *marché* buzzed with activity in the dawn light. Merchants were opening up their stores, displaying wares on their small patio entryways—plastic buckets; foam mattresses; fashionable clothing from Libreville, which came in by truck or barge the day before. Tailors set out several of their best traditional outfits to entice fashion-conscious folks into their salons. And the mamas set up their fruit and vegetable stands, flush with plantains, mangoes, papaya, chile peppers, and manioc.

A few fishermen headed up from the lagoon to sell fresh-caught Capitaine and barracuda, perch and tilapia. Some set up their old iceboxes along the side of the main street, with rickety scales to weigh kilos and make their sales. Others headed over to the local fishermen's cooperative, which asked a small membership fee but offered storage space in massive, electric freezers, allowing the fishermen to rest assured that their fish would be sold, without each individual having to conduct the sale under the hot sun.

Other fishermen came in with smoked and dried fish by the boxful, packaged and ready to load up onto the next transport headed into the interior, toward Tchibanga. The steady stream of commerce running back and forth between Gamba and Tchibanga normally ran as follows: fish (smoked, dried, or frozen) left Gamba in exchange for enormous quantities of plantains, bananas, and other fruit coming in from Tchibanga. And all of this was conducted via *taxi-brousse* (bush taxis).

One of the normal transport specialists, whom I only knew as Mamadou, owned an old pickup truck with a metal-framed enclosure in the bed. On one particular morning, he packed that bed full of fish, chickens, random bags of who-knows-what, and luggage; and finally, piled on top of all of this cargo, he started loading in people. Unlike my friend Demsey's truck, this pickup was not an extended cab.

Mamadou would pack in two, three, four passengers into the cab, usually children or women, and then he would sell space in the bed of the truck on top of the chickens and plantains to everyone else. Ten, twelve, fifteen, even twenty people could pile in, holding onto the metal frame, sitting on uncomfortable piles of fruit and fish; and occasionally, to the consternation of the crowded-in passengers, Mamadou would load in a goat, which would stand on top of everything and everyone like a furry, horned, ornery king of the hill.

Not many people own vehicles in Gabon, so those brave souls who know (or think they know) how to drive on the remote roads of the country are able to make a small fortune transporting goods and people (and goats) from one place to another. And for some reason, Gabonese often dress up in their best clothes to travel, even when they risk long dusty days—or soaking wet ones.

Most of my travels around Gamba, including on the road to Tchibanga, were with joint missions of education and conservation individuals, so I was able to enjoy somewhat less jam-packed (in terms of people and cargo) trips in a WWF Land Cruiser or a European Union pickup. But I did occasionally snag a ride on a *taxi-brousse*, jammed in with everyone and everything, headed to Tchibanga, or, if a driver had the day off, to Setté Cama.

People, including many of my Peace Corps colleagues, were used to traveling in these crazy transports, packed in like sardines, or more appropriately, fruit and dried fish. In August 2003 I experienced my most memorable (and painful) experience in a *taxi-brousse*. I was participating in a training session for the new Peace Corps volunteers who came in a year after my group, in the town of Koulamoutou. This town is located in the Ogooué-Lolo Province, in central-eastern Gabon. It is a beautiful town situated on the Lolo River. Jean Pierre had accompanied me to help show the new Peace Corps volunteers how he and I worked together to co-teach environmental education classes.

After our part of the training was completed, Jean Pierre had to leave earlier than me, so a group of Peace Corps Volunteers from my *stage* (the group that started at the same time as I did) and I decided to go visit several volunteers living in the mountain town of Iboundji. We grabbed our bags and headed out to a *taxi-brousse* stop on the road that led out of town toward Iboundji. We bought some cookies and Coca-Cola to drink while we waited for the next transport. And we waited, and waited. And waited.

Finally, after what I remember as being several hours, a pickup truck pulled up, full of people and cargo. I don't remember the price of the ride (it was not much), but I do remember cramming in to the back of the truck, which, like Mamadou's truck, had a metal cage and roll bar. There were probably fifteen people already sitting and standing amidst the bulky bags of clothes and food. And off we went.

We left a little after noon, with the dust billowing all around. I was thrilled at the experience, standing in the back of the truck, comfortable with the knowledge that no roads could be anywhere as difficult or bouncy as the road between Gamba and Tchibanga. We started climbing, and the road got steeper. From time to time, the driver would stop to let people off as they headed to their plantations, or to pick up other folks waiting (some for hours) on the side of the road. The road started to get pretty bumpy, though not as bad as near Gamba, I kept telling myself. Each bump would throw the entire conglomerated jumble of people and luggage around, banging knees and stomachs, arms and legs. I held firmly to the metal bars, trying to minimize my surface area within the chaos.

Then, all thought of the difficulty of the roads of Gamba left my head. The driver stopped to let off some passengers at a particularly steep part of the road. Or at least, he tried to stop. He had a young boy helping him load and unload gear and passengers, and at this point, the boy took on another task. He would jump from the side of the truck where he was hanging on precariously with a set of heavy pieces of wood, which he would then run down the hill and place under the back two tires as the truck started to roll backwards. And roll it did, with all of us weighing it down.

Then, once the truck came to a semi-stop on these now tiny-seeming pieces of wood, the passengers would get on or off, and the driver would hit the gas and lumber his way up the hill. The boy would grab the pieces of wood, which I now saw were attached by a yellow twine, and race uphill after us until he could grab onto the side of the metal cage. The going was so slow that it soon became dark. And this semi-stop, roll back, wood under the tires, loading, unloading, bouncing around, continued for hours. At one point, as I gripped the metal bars for dear life, I felt a snap in one of the bars after we hit a big pothole. No one else seemed to mind, but I feared that the whole cage would come apart and fly away, along with me.

After what seemed like days, we reached Iboundji. I staggered off the back of the truck with my friends toward their homes near the Iboundji school. The next morning, when we finally were able to see the town, I also noticed that my legs were completely banged up; my thighs were black and blue from bruises and sore from standing upright against the rickety metal bars of the *taxi-brousse* for so many hours. *I'll take those Gamba roads any day*, I thought.

Iboundji is a small community situated on Mount Iboundji, the tallest mountain in Gabon. It is forested, with tracks of cleared land serving as space for nearby villages and the actual town. We spent the day exploring the town, as my friends showed us where they lived and worked. They did not have electricity or water, so we followed as they walked over a half-mile to a stream with buckets, then back up hill to their homes where they would boil and filter the water. Bathing was conducted along this same beautiful little stream.

We happened to be in Iboundji for Gabonese Independence Day, the 17 août (August 17), a Sunday in 2003. We attended an official parade and later visited a family further up the mountain, friends of my Peace Corps colleagues. We sat and talked with the older men in this family, including several inebriated dancers, one who claimed to be a Pygmy married to a Bantu woman. Whether his claim was true or not, he was certainly much shorter than his wife (and everyone else).

I enjoyed visiting Iboundji, despite the ride up the mountain. On our final morning, we were able to catch a ride with a local dignitary who had a nearly empty pickup. This time, the ride down the mountain was much quicker, less jam-packed, even pleasant. Now, wherever I am, my bar for the difficulty of a road is measured not just with the adventurous route between Tchibanga and Gamba, but also with the treacherous mountain trek up to Iboundji.

Palm Wine

My glass sat perched on the small wooden table, covered by a plastic checkered tablecloth. In the center of the table sat a large bottle filled with a thick, light yellow liquid, milky and topped off with dirty white foam and flecks of brown, dried bark. Around the table sat my mother, father, and two brothers. We had just returned to Libreville after spending nearly two weeks in and around Gamba town, where I had shown them some of what life on the Ndougou Lagoon, surrounded by forest, is like. I was joining them on a short jaunt to South Africa, and we were staying in the capital for a night before our flight in the morning.

While touring around Libreville, taking in sights such as the wonderfully carved wooden columns at L'Eglise Saint Michel (St. Michael's Church), I asked our taxi driver to take us to a roadside bar where we could drink some *vin de palme*, or *toutou*. He smiled and said his cousin had just such a spot.

Turning down a gravel alley, dusty and dry in the mild heat of midafternoon (this was during the *grande saison sèche*), he pulled up across from a makeshift auto repair shop, where a small wooden shack sat with a few tables underneath an old mango tree.

"*On y est,*" he said. "We're here."

And indeed, we were. A counter attached to the shack was filled with large plastic and glass bottles, all full of the whitish-yellow liquid. I ordered up a bottle and some glasses, explaining to the bartender that this was the first time my family would be trying palm wine. The other patrons smiled knowingly, waiting to see the expressions on the faces of my brothers and parents as they took their first sips of this traditional drink.

I poured out a small amount in everyone's glasses, explaining that palm wine was a must-try experience and that Gabonese families prided themselves on the quality of their wine. *Vin de palme* is made by fermenting the liquidy sap of a palm tree, such as the raffia palm or the oil palm. The sap of the palm tree is either tapped, usually from the top of the tree, in a manner similar to tapping for maple syrup, or a tree is cut down, tilted at an angle with a bore hole, and drained of its sweet liquid. Often, the fermenting takes place in huge, round green jars, stoppered with either a cork or even a piece of cloth. The sweet liquid from the tree is left to sit, and the vintner then adds in his desired amount of dried, powdered, bitter wood or bark to cut the sweetness and render the wine more palatable.

I encouraged everyone to first smell the wine, to understand that the slightly acidic odor was due to the fermented palm sap and added flavoring. Then I took the first drink. From my own experience, this wine was not too bad. It was thick, but not too sweet or overly bitter. I drank slowly, enjoying the refreshing flavor and relaxed atmosphere at the palm wine bar.

My mother tried just a tiny drop, as she is not fond of most alcoholic beverages. Her eyes widened, and her lips pursed tightly shut. Shaking her head, she said that was enough for her. Then my father drank from his glass, his eyes narrowing and his nostrils flaring slightly. He smiled sourly and shook his head, saying, "Interesting flavor; must be an acquired taste."

The other customers all laughed, having expected such a reaction. And then my brothers tried their glasses. Spencer, my youngest brother, had a reaction similar to my father's, but he shrugged and finished his glass. Ian bravely took up his cup, swirled the contents and held it up so as to see where the floating pieces of wood sat, before tilting back his head and taking a swig. Sputtering, he looked around and said wryly, "This is like drinking rancid peanut butter."

In the Ndougou Lagoon region of Gabon, most of the palm wine that I tried was the same bitter drink my family was unable to appreciate. And while *toutou* is definitely an acquired taste, the strength, bitterness or sweetness, and taste all depend on the method by which the wine is made.

Palm wine is served at parties, ceremonies, on the side of the road, and in nearly every village I ever visited. It is a traditional substitute for harder alcohol; it is much cheaper to make and purchase. The alcohol content and effects on humans are similar to the effects of grape wines and grain alcohols.[6] A drink that often accompanies *vin de palme*, at least at wedding ceremonies, is *musungu*, a wine made from fermented honey. I enjoyed this seemingly rarer beverage only a few times, and like honey beer and wine in other parts of the world, the taste of syrupy mead was usually too sweet for my preferences.

After explaining how the wine was made and the importance of *vin de palme* in many Gabonese ceremonies, I finished my glass. We still had about half a bottle of wine left before us, and the taxi driver was content waiting for a few more minutes, laughing with his cousin at these foreigners trying to drink his wine. I asked if I could top off anyone's glasses, and my mother and brothers declined. My father said he would finish what he had left, but he would leave the rest to me. I filled my glass for another round, but left some liquid in the bottle, not wanting to overindulge.

Over the next several years, I grew to appreciate differences in *vin de palme*, to notice textural varieties, vintner preferences in bitterness or sweetness, and the joy a family had in serving a drink they had grown, brewed, and shared. And although not everyone actually enjoys drinking *toutou*, the fact that it is made in Gabon is a source of great pride in tradition and culture. And although I do not believe it ever became my favorite drink, I miss being able to sit down in the village to share a bottle of Setté Cama *vin de palme* with my friends.

*Jean Pierre Bayet with Ibonga students at a Setté Cama village
chief's palm wine plantation*

Dancing to the Drums

Darkness jumped out of the fading twilight with confidence, settling on the still-heated village of Setté Cama like an old jacket—zipped up, keeping the warmth in but the light out. Mosquitos, however, were not kept out. The scream-buzz of the female anopheles beat at my eardrums, nearly drowning out a muted drumbeat coming from somewhere out in the obscurity. The night smelled of wood fire and hot peppers and onions, as the neighbors heated their fish stew in an old worn pot. I had just awoken from a nap in Jean Pierre's lagoonside house, where I was staying for the weekend, to find the house empty.

The faraway drums seemed to reverberate along with my mosquito-influenced hearing, sinking down into my bones. Thrum, dumm dumm, followed by ricocheted taps. Faster, deeper, beckoning. It was the Earth's heartbeat, strong, palpitating, constant, but varied. It called to me.

So I went. I slowly made my way along the sandy path, conscious of the desire to start tapping my hands in time with the beat. One foot placed down in the darkness, followed by the other, making my way around the now-quiet village homes. The people were already out there, with the drums.

As I walked along, almost in a trance, I thought back to my first experience with drumming in Gabon. During my initial three-month stay in Lambaréné, learning about the work I would be doing, the culture, and really just setting the stage for my introduction to the country, I lived with a wonderful host family, the Engeng Nguema family, on the left bank of the Ogooué River.

One evening, similar to the one I now walked through, my host brother, Julien, led me along a dark, sandy path toward a glowing clearing, in front of someone's home. A large group of people formed a circle around the cleared space, watching, waiting. I moved closer to the edge of this group, wondering what was going to happen. Bam, tap tap tap, thrummmmm. A man sitting under a small tree near a bonfire at the clearing's center started to speak through the drum. It seemed to build and build, until suddenly two shapes appeared from the darkness. (I suspect they came from the other side of the home, but at the time, they looked to have stepped through some otherworldly portal.)

These shapes were covered in long, yellow hair, with frightening white faces poking out of the top of the limp fur. They held palm fronds tightly, and as the drums continued, they began to dance, whirling from one foot to the other, slapping the fronds on the ground. Circling the clearing, they edged closer and closer to the crowd. Some watchers began to chant in time with the drums, or so it seemed to me. My entire being was transfixed by the mysterious creatures.

I was a fair bit taller than the folks of Lambaréné, and these creatures approached my height. I could see bare feet protruding out from beneath what I came to see were long, dry strands of raffia, a plant common to many parts of the world, which can be woven into clothing. As I looked closer, I knew these were men, dressed in some kind of costume, with a wooden mask set atop. But looking even closer, how could I be sure?

Suddenly, one of the creatures rushed a section of the crowd. People fell back with screams. Children clutched their parents, and a gasping chant whispered some kind of warning message I could not comprehend. It circled back into the middle, whipping that palm frond on the ground. Then, it stopped. It stopped and the drums stopped. And all eyes turned to look at the tall, pale intruder standing in my shoes. The spirit-being pointed its whip at me, and the drums started up once more, much faster. The thing rushed at me, bouncing from foot to foot until it stood dancing and pointing and growling, a foot in front of my face. I froze, unable to move and afraid to even try. Julien came to stand beside me, calmly stating that I was with him. The demon threw its hairy arms toward the inky sky and fever-danced back into the clearing, matching the intensity of the drums.

Then, two men came out of the house. They took the fronds from the beasts and started moving to the tam, tam, thrumm, swinging the fronds with even more ferocity than the creatures. And "thwack," they each hit the back of a monster. They beat the creatures as they danced, and the monsters roared and danced and were beaten down to the ground. They gave a final surge each, moving with what seemed like a million flashing feet, kicking up sand and twirling; then they fell down and moved no more. The drums kept on, and the men chanted and the crowd answered. They would utter a proclamation, and the response came strongly, "Hungh." More people came from the house, and the drums softened. I could hear crying inside now. The people picked up the defeated beasts and carried them inside.

One old man came up to me and told me in hushed, broken French that I had to follow the group inside, but that if I did, I would never be seen or heard from again. I looked at my host brother, and he motioned for me to ignore the old man and led me back home.

Julien explained to me the following morning that a neighbor had died several days before, and the dance and drums had scared out the neighbor's spirit so that his family could convince him to move on from this world. I suspect some of the ritual, at least the part aimed at me, was simply part of the performance, meant to scare the intruder (me) and provide some levity in an otherwise somber occasion. To this day, that drumming and the dancing creatures still haunt my dreams.

Thoughts of that first drumming pursued me back to the present evening, and as I walked toward the ever-increasing pounding along the forest path, I could not help but wonder what I was being led into. Would a raffia beast be waiting again?

A fire glow echoed off the trees and slowly brought into silhouette a friend's home at the edge of the village. Shadows played across the walls of the structure, jagged and wispy at the same time. These shadow-beings were absorbed by the trees. I stepped off of the path, into the glow of a small fire, around which all the village youth were dancing in a circle, swaying and dipping and laughing. Two drummers were flashing hands across the leather drum heads; one sat on a massive, six-foot-long drum, producing a deep, rumbling bass. The other sat on a log and played a round, bongo-type drum with intricate rhythm and speed. They spoke through the drums, directly to my quivering, shaking soul. "Join us," they seemed to say.

When the dancers saw me, they called for me to join the circle. Jean Pierre was already there, and he told me that this dance was called the *Ekounda*. It was about having fun and was allowed for boys and girls, men and women. Many other dances and rituals in Gabon are reserved for single-gender groups, for members who have followed secret initiations. But *Ekounda* could be danced even by the likes of me. So I joined, attempting to imitate the swaying to the drums.

Then one person jumped into the middle of the circle, feet flying and swirling around and over the fire. Laughing, until—stop—he or she would freeze, then gesture toward another in the surrounding circle, challenging that person to top his or her dance. One could gesture with the hands, feet, hips, elbows. One could pretend to be bored and point to one's watch like it was time to go. It was great fun!

Jean Pierre took a turn in the middle, breaking into some kind of country line dance (he loved reminding me that his

50

favorite musicians include Don Williams and Kenny Rogers; I suspected that a former Peace Corps volunteer had given Jean Pierre a couple of country tapes years earlier). He stopped, smiled, and pointed at me to take my turn.

I rushed into the middle and started my best interpretation of a whirling Dervish, hopping over the fire and spinning in midair. The crowd roared with laughter and encouragement. Both were certainly needed. Then a friend joked that I had better turn the center over to someone else before I fell in the fire. Smiling in agreement, I stopped, gestured toward a section of the crowd with my elbow and rejoined the circle, swaying (out of tempo) to the hypnotic drumming. Tam, tam tam tam. Thrummmm.

Part II: Lessons from Lambaréné

You do not live in a world all alone. Your brothers are here too.

You must give some time to your fellow men. Even if it's a little thing, do something for others—something for which you get no pay but the privilege of doing it.

—ALBERT SCHWEITZER

Mon Frère le Nganga

⌖

T here are so many characteristics about a place, a people, a culture, that remain hidden from the outsider, that an interloper, even one who lives in a place for years at a time, may never come to know. The secret spot to hang out where all the locals go, versus the tourist traps; the stories that are never discussed but everyone who was born there knows. For me, initiation rites in Gabon are one of these mysterious, never-fully-understood characteristics, those secrets that are mentioned briefly but never fully explained.

In Gabon, there are many different sects, or secret societies, geared mostly at helping initiates work together to overcome challenges, such as sickness, community decisions, and other problems. Some are limited to men, others to women. In fact, the women who owned the home I rented in Gamba town were all part of the Niembe (or Njembe) society, which conducted healing ceremonies and traditional funerals.[7] Many aspects of these rites are visible to the uninitiated; notably, the dancing, drumming, singing, and days-long ceremonies that occurred fifty feet from my front door. However, the rituals of the initiates are exactly those...only for initiates.

Many Gabonese belong to one society or another, but for those uninitiated, whether Gabonese or not, each society is steeped in rumor, mystery, and magic. And the most celebrated, even feared, society of men is Bwiti. Like Niembe, Bwiti is thought to help teach healing powers to its initiates, to assist them in understanding who they are and where they come from, to commune with their spiritual selves and those of their ancestors. Initiates undergo various rites in which they ingest a good quantity of *iboga*, which is a bitter-tasting root thought to possess healing and shamanistic powers. From personal experience, *iboga* is a strong stimulant, like caffeine on overdrive. It helps one to stay awake on long walks in the forest, or presumably, during the long initiation ceremonies.

In Bwiti, the principal healer is called a *Nganga* (pronounced "nnn GAN ga"). This term has come to mean many things to many people, from witchdoctor to herbalist, from traditional healer to shaman. The *Nganga* is the initiate who can help either initiate others or help them with their health problems, as well as, presumably, conjure up curses and maledictions.

When I arrived at our Peace Corps training site, in the town of Lambaréné, I was adopted by the Endeng Nguema family, of the Fang ethnicity. My host brother, Julien, was, he claimed, a *Nganga*. Julien explained to me that he had a near-debilitating illness as a child, which partially crippled one of his feet. (I always suspected it was something like polio.) His family took him to see a traditional healer (another *Nganga*), and Julien was healed through a lengthy initiation. He said he learned how to differentiate between many different plants in the forest, what their properties were, and how to use them to help people. And he said he wanted to initiate me.

Julien Endeng Nguema dressed as a Nganga in Lambaréné

While excited at the prospect of learning so much about Gabonese culture and Bwiti in particular, I told him I wanted to think about it and wondered if it would be alright for me to ask him questions before making up my mind. He readily agreed.

According to Julien, Bwiti was originally a religion discovered by the Baka Pygmies deep in the forest. It was then taken up by the Bantu peoples, including his people, the Fang. He said that good initiates focused on helping others, on teaching about the past and tradition to encourage good living in the present. However, he also said that some people abused the powers they gained through initiation and used them for evil purposes.

As part of the specific training the environmental education volunteers were given, a group of us spent a few nights with another volunteer, who had already been in Gabon for a year and lived and worked in the town of Booué, outside of Lopé National Park. Around ten of us piled into her house and put our sleeping bags, blankets, and sheets on the floor. In the middle of the night, I awoke to hear one of the other trainees breathing heavily in the next room. Another trainee got up to (I assume) use the restroom; the hard-breathing trainee seemed to return to normal sleep breathing, and I went back to sleep.

The next morning, one trainee explained that she had had a very bad experience during the night. She said she woke up in the middle of the night and noticed that everyone around her was fast asleep. She then looked around the room and noticed that a light seemed to be coming from outside the wooden planks of the home, like a flashlight in someone's hand.

Slowly at first, then more quickly, the light seemed to push through the wall, until it was like an independently moving spirit inside the home. She said she felt paralyzed, and then she seemed to see a shadow, like a person standing at her feet. This shadow seemed to reach down and grab her, and started pulling her by her feet. She explained that she somehow knew that if she was pulled far enough, she would be dead.

As she sat, paralyzed and terrified, one of the other women trainees lying next to her got up and left the room, and the shadow being and strange light disappeared. She then fell back asleep.

When I got back to my host family's home in Lambaréné, I relayed the story to Julien. He frowned in thought and then nodded. He explained that someone had wanted to test the foreigners, to see what we were made of, and had used his powers to send in an evil presence. He said that in Gabon, many people called this *le vampirisme* (vampirism), a word adopted from the French because the malevolent spirit would suck the life away from the unwary sleeper. These people could send their spirits out on what he called *voyages nocturne* (nocturnal journeys) or on an *avion nocturne* (a mystical night airplane) anywhere in the world to affect others in their sleep.[8] According to Julien, the safest way to keep such spirits (whether sent by magic airplane or not) away in the middle of the night was to place a lit candle in a bottle of water in your bedroom. He said the light would attract any evil presences, and the water would trap them.

I later told this trick to my fellow trainees. In fact, after experiencing a similar being hovering over my feet when I first got to my post in Gamba, I used the candle-in-water trick a few times. Some of you may laugh and say that I was probably having a nightmare, based on the memory of my fellow trainee's story. That may be the case, but when in Gabon, one tends to go with what the locals believe. And hey, it worked; I was never bothered again by the evil presence.

In any case, Julien assured me that most *Ngangas* use their skills for good. I asked him what that meant, and here is what I remember him saying:

As a *Nganga*, I am able to see into a person to determine whether they have a sickness. I can tell when someone has the *loa loa* [a filarial nematode that lives beneath the skin and can even swim across the eye] or when someone has cancer. I then know which herbs can help relieve the pain or, in some cases, which combination of traditional medicine can help heal the person. And this knowledge comes from the knowledge of generations of *Nganga*, which you learn through the Bwiti initiation ceremony and through practice.

Intrigued, I asked more about the knowledge from previous generations. My host brother explained that while undergoing the initiation ceremony, one was placed on a woven mat in the middle of the *corps de garde*, which is usually a raffia- or palm-roofed, open-air "temple."[9] These *corps de garde* can also sometimes serve as community meeting places. All around the initiate, torches made from banana leaves and bark, filled with sap from vines and trees, burned, and musicians invoked the ancestors through song, dance, and music from an instrument called a *mongongo* and the drum.

The initiators would then bring a drink full of bitter *iboga* for the initiate to drink, and they would recant the history of Bwiti through the ages as the *iboga* took hold and transported the initiate back to the beginning, when the ancestors first found Bwiti in the forest. And after a certain amount of time, sometimes days, the ceremony was finished, and the initiate came back with the knowledge and wisdom of the ages.

Having spent many evenings in discussions with Julien, and seeing how others treated him, it was evident that he possessed an old soul, full of wisdom and experience. His neighbors respected him, treated him like an elder, even though he was no older than I was. All because he was a *Nganga*.

Eventually, I declined the invitation to become initiated myself. This was mostly because I had hyperanalyzed the ceremony and the effect of *iboga* on my brain, wherein it acts like a stimulant such that I was not surprised to hear that most initiates came away with the same experience of the ancestors. This result seemed to me to be unavoidable, given Julien's description of the initiators whispering into his ears while the *iboga* took effect. My ultimate reason for declining was because I did not want to disrespect the tradition with my overanalytical, perhaps jaded perspective. Still, I am proud of *mon frère de Lambaréné*, one of the celebrated *Nganga* of Gabon.

Mongongo

I placed the arc, like a bow strung tightly with a thin, dried vine, between my legs. Seated on an old bench, I watched for cues from Julien. He showed me solemnly how to hold my left hand close to the tip of the thick, arched wood so that I held it steady while allowing my fingers to grasp and move a smaller piece of wood, rounded like a fat, miniature drum stick. With my right hand, I held on to a thin, long stick, straight like an arrow. This thinner stick was just long enough to reach from the lowest bend in the arc slightly over the vine string holding the bow in its curved position.

Nervously, I bent my head down slightly and opened my mouth around the thin vine, keeping my lips close enough to hover above and below the vine string. And then, mouth open and quivering, I started to tap the string with the stick in my right hand, forming a haphazard rhythm that sounded slightly like strumming a single, muted guitar string. With my left hand, I alternated between pushing on the vine with the fat stick and letting up, changing the pitch of my rhythm.

Slowly, the sound seemed to reach down into my throat, pulling at my vocal cords and echoing softly back out into the night air. I kept at it, tapping and pushing, trying to keep my mouth from actually touching the vine string. After a few minutes, I looked up and saw Julien smiling. "*Bien fait, mon frère*," he told me. "Well done, my brother."

Julien teaching Peace Corps Volunteers to play the mongongo

A love of music was something Julien and I had in common, and while he taught me some of playing the bow-like instrument, I taught him how to play the guitar I had brought with me to Gabon.

Now, in listening to his teachings, I felt giddy, having seen him perform on this simple, mystical, wonderful instrument and wanting to give it a go of my own. Of course, the sound (and rhythm) I generated was tiny, unpracticed, and unimpressive, but I thought I was getting the hang of how it worked. With a big smile of my own, I handed the arc and sticks back to Julien, asking him to play some real music. He took back his instrument and sat down to play.

This instrument is a *mongongo*, or a musical arc (called *arc musical* in French). It is infused with a sacred quality in its simplicity, natural materials, and the haunting sounds it produces. A *mongongo* is often the first instrument to start playing in traditional ceremonies and songs, with the musician leading a group of drummers in hours-long initiation rites and other rituals.

Julien explained to me that he had made this *mongongo* himself, picking out the right thickness of vine, or *liane*, at the right moment, so that he could bend it without risk of breaking. He judged the moisture in the *liane* so perfectly that the bend held, exactly the same as the stave of a hunting bow. Next, he gathered a much thinner, stringier *liane* with which to draw the stave. He also picked out the thin rhythm stick from the stem of a small bush near where the vines came from, cutting off leaf buds and smoothing it out by hand, as well as the pitch-changing piece of wood, which he attached to one end of the instrument with leftover *liane* string. The *mongongo* was ready to play.

Settling down with ease, Julien began to sing through those vines. He hypnotized me with his simple tapping rhythm, creating a constant reverberation, with an expertly timed pitch change here, and here, and there. And then the sound drove into him, past his lips and into his throat, where it seemed to grow, expand, and shoot back out to my waiting ears. The rhythmic tapping played off of his vocal cords, changing slightly as he added this much more complicated human instrument into the mix. With slight movements of his throat, he was able to bring out more sound from that *mongongo* than I thought possible, all the while avoiding any touch of his lips to the vine string. It reminded me somewhat of the Australian didgeridoo, a wind instrument that sings with a gravelly echo. So this *mongongo* changed from a simple forest string instrument into a string, wind, and spiritual sound.

Then, when I thought he had reached the limits of his already impressive musical skills, Julien began to sing, to actually move words and sound out of his lungs while simultaneously pulling the rhythm in and pushing it out with his vocal cords. He sang quietly, but clearly and strongly over the other sounds of the *arc musical*. Later, Julien told me that he was only just learning how to sing separately, but concurrently, while playing, and that the most expert musicians could seem to be two separate people at the same time. This only further impressed upon me the hypnotic, spiritual nature of the *mongongo*, and I understood why the instrument is so valued throughout Gabon. It serves as a musical divining rod, which can separate a person from himself while somehow still holding him together.

Gabon is a country full of musical wonders, from expert drummers to stringed instruments such as the *mongongo* and the *sitar*.[10] There are innumerable dance and singing troupes, musicians for hire, and musicians generally. And the sounds of these instruments, especially the drums and the *mongongo*, echo through the forest. One of the few regrets I have from my time in the forests of Gabon is that I was not able to learn more of playing the *mongongo* or other instruments essential to Gabonese history, tradition, and culture. But to that regret, all I can say is, play on Julien, play on....

17 Août

The light gray clouds hovered above, swirling slowly sometimes with a soft breeze, but often sitting stagnant in the sky. They were low and heavy, seemingly full of rain, yet afraid to open up. It was the middle of the *grande saison sèche*, which normally lasts from May through September. Although the clouds looked like rain, the air was dry, dusty. The red laterite road spewed fine particles into the air like a geyser, billowing behind every passing vehicle. Each footstep kicked up smaller bubbles of dust, caking my nose and throat. On days like this one, it was easy to forget the difficulties caused by the rainy seasons, when the dust turned to thick, chunky, sticky mud.

The stores around the *marché* in Lambaréné were hopping, brightly lit, and bellowing their music from grainy-sounding stereo systems into the local atmosphere. All around town, I could see small Gabonese flags, green, yellow, and blue, hanging from homes and stores; and the government prefecture flew the flag high in the nearly windless day. August...dry, cool, and perhaps, above all, festive.

As I continued walking along the narrow side of the road, I could not help noticing how happy people were, smiling and carrying on with a hurried grace, as if trying to rush slowly, not ready to give up the nonchalance of normal days but acutely aware that today was a day not to be late. Many townspeople wore shirts depicting President Bongo Ondimba, stern yet proud with his sleek glasses and close-cropped hair. Above him, the words *Partie Démocratique du Gabon* (PDG for short) were written in blue and green, standing out on the white T-shirts. The PDG was the major party in Gabon, the president's party. And his supporters were fervent and many.

These T-shirts, the flags, and the loud music signified Independence Day in Gabon, the seventeenth of August, le *17 août*. Gabon gained independence from France in 1960, following a peaceful turnover by the French to then-President Léon Mba. Omar Bongo, after serving as vice-president, succeeded President Mba in 1967 and served as Gabon's president until his death in 2009. The *17 août* of 2002 was the first independence day I experienced in Gabon.

Although many of the stores in the *marché* were open for a few hours on this day, most businesses were closed for the holiday. Families would get together for food, drink, laughter, political discussions, and remembrance. The celebrations may have lacked the expensive fireworks of a Fourth of July ceremony in the United States, but the spirit of unity and festivity was certainly not lacking throughout Gabon. On this day, everyone was proud to be Gabonese, from the local folks to the expatriated foreigners. The green, yellow, and blue were omnipresent.

I continued walking along the dusty road, heading home from a Peace Corps get-together near my host family's home in the neighborhood of *Isaac*. Not far from home, Julien met me and invited me to a neighbor's yard, where food was being prepared, drinks were being chilled on ice, and music was already playing. Someone had lent them fifty-plus red and white plastic chairs, and by the time I arrived, children were already playing and running around the sandy terrain, while the women cooked chicken, plantains, and rice, and the men helped with the stereo system and the bottles of Régab beer and palm wine.

Julien spotted some friends, already in deep discussion and laughter. We pulled up a chair and joined them. Everyone waved at everyone else, smiling and wishing each other a *bonne fête*, cajoling one another about a recent failed attempt to seek a date with one of the bartenders in town, or discussing the pros and cons of different fishing methods.

All of this activity, except for some of the cooking, occurred under the cloudy sky. While it constantly looked like rain, one could be fairly certain for those months in the middle of the *grande saison sèche* that it would not rain; hence the ease of setting up a party for several dozen people without putting up tents or tarpaulins.

Children would occasionally come over to our little group and others, asking if anyone would like more food or drink, much of which had been paid for by the organizing committee of the PDG in Lambaréné. Most politicians were of this political party, and celebrations around town, around the province, and around the country were similarly sponsored—this sponsorship also sometimes included gifts of those T-shirts many people were wearing, the ones with the president's face plastered all over them.

And so, similar to independence days around the world, the *17 août* was a time of national reflection, national dialogue, and, most evidently, national celebration. I learned much of the recent history of the country, from colonialism, which all of the elders remembered, to the one-party rule that lasted from 1963 to 1990, to the current several-party system in which only the PDG has any real power. I heard praise and objections to President Bongo, equally heated, yet nearly professorially debated, perhaps because of my presence. And I was impressed by the civic knowledge nearly everyone possessed. Everyone seemed to know the history of their local, provincial, and national political machinations. They knew (sometimes personally) their elected officials, as well as the history of those officials, which families they came from, and how they rose to and fell from power.

This *17 août* served as a lesson to me of the importance of knowing and remembering the people and politics of a place, the engagement of a population in its own governance, no matter how tenuous. So on the next *17 août*, as well as the next Fourth of July, I will try to remember the feeling of citizenship I experienced in Gabon; the sense of the individual belonging with the whole, not just in the present, but also in the past, glimpsed through the eyes of the existing generations, looking back as well as forward. *Bonne fête oh!*

Lambaréné fish market on Ogooué River

Practice Garden

"**C**an you pass me that shovel, please?"

After wiping my brow with a bandana, I handed the long, wooden-handled shovel over to my fellow trainee. Most of our training, prior to becoming full-fledged Peace Corps Volunteers, took place at a school on the big hill on the *rive droite* (right bank) of the Ogooué River. A mile or so uphill from this school, hidden away by homes and winding footpaths, and tucked away in a ravine, was a farm where one of the host families had agreed to allow the environmental education trainees to learn a little bit about Gabonese agricultural practices.

The farm had sloping hills, covered by sparse grasses and trees full of yellow cacao pods, those hanging fruits that hide future chocolate sauce in thick seeds. Weedlike pineapples grew haphazardly out of spiked leaf clumps. The hills dropped down onto a flatter section of land, with shrubs and felled trunks of various tree species. Manioc sprouted in short rows of thick stalks with light green leaves sitting on top like miniature umbrellas. Large-leafed taro plants and sweet and plantain banana trees dotted the farm as well.

In the center of the flat land, the farmer was lecturing roughly twenty environmental education trainees on the importance of well-tilled soil and raised beds, of planting seeds and watering them with care. The spot, having been cleared of trees and shrubs and crops, overflowed with clumpy, reddish dirt. This was our practice garden.

Over the course of several weeks, we cut away the grass and shrubs with machetes and dug at the soil with shovels, until we had enough dirt to form rectangular mounds. These we shaped side by side, leaving enough room to walk between them, six or seven in total. With shovels and machetes, hoes and rakes, we spread the mounds out to be roughly five feet wide and ten feet long. We created our first Gabonese raised beds.

The Peace Corps trainers had provided us with packets of seeds—tomatoes, carrots, plants we were all familiar with from back home. In town, we found seeds for green beans, okra, and the spicy peppers that grew well in Gabon. A few of us tried planting lettuce and cabbage, green leafy delicacies which were hard to come by in Lambaréné. Each bed was claimed by three or four trainees, and we took on the semi-serious challenge of competing against each other to see whose crops grew best. Our trainers and the farmer egged us on, imparting various tidbits of wisdom about the importance of well-planted, well-grown food.

Throughout our time in Lambaréné, we took turns watering the beds, hauling plastic watering cans up to the pump and then back down the hill to our little spot of sprouting greens. Holding two cans, one could water two beds at once, walking slowly while emptying the life-giving liquid over the shoots and roots of our future meals.

Since this was the *grande saison sèche*, the long dry season, this water was essential, because the rains wouldn't be coming for several months, and when they finally did, they could wash away any plants that weren't already firmly established. So we tended our practice garden with care, following instructions from the farmer, and hoping to see the fruits (and vegetables) of our labor before the end of our training.

In constructing our garden, the farmer told us that one of the most important measures we needed to take, one which could prove essential should we decide to try our hands at gardening alone in our eventual permanent postings throughout the country, was the construction of a sturdy, protective fence around the entire garden. These fences would keep out bush pigs, stray dogs, and other animals, though larger forest creatures like elephants could probably just push on through.

Having grown up in Montana, in a family that kept horses, I was experienced at building fences—barbed-wire fences, with metal and wooden fence posts; sturdy wooden fences, with deep-set railroad ties for posts; electric-wire fences to keep the horses away from near the family cabin. I had practice using augers, shovels, post-pounders, picks, hoes, spades, clamshells, wire splitters and tighteners, hammers and nails, metal posts and wooden ones. I joked with my fellow trainees that this was one task I knew I was up to and that I looked forward to seeing whether the farmer could teach me anything new.

On the day we started building the fence, we had just finished shaping the raised beds and hadn't yet planted anything. I didn't know what kind of material the farmer would suggest we use, but I thought I was ready for anything.

Off to the side of our mounds lay a pile of slim-cut tree trunks and thick bamboo stalks, long and green and hollow. *This bamboo will never hold a nail,* I thought, *but perhaps we'll plant a few, then string the others up with some kind of twine.* Sure enough, the farmer had us dig holes at the outside corners of our arrayed mounds of dirt.

As I handed the shovel to one of my friends, I grabbed another. I began digging in the hard dirt, forming a hole that would be large enough to place a bamboo stalk or tree branch or trunk in, pack rocks around it for stability and strength, and fill it back in with the dirt. Some of my colleagues gathered rocks from around the farm, and we packed that corner post tightly. So far, so good.

Our Peace Corps trainer told us we were doing great, and had us dig and plant a few more posts (both bamboo and cut wood) around the perimeter of the garden. When we had a sufficient structure, I looked around for some barbed wire, or for some kind of filler that could be attached to the hollow posts. Several other trainees were doing the same search I was, but we did not find anything.

The trainers laughed, clearly in cahoots with the farmer. They turned around and pointed at the remaining pile of bamboo stalks.

"How are we supposed to use those to close this fence in?" I asked. "Do you mean we have to dig more holes and simply surround the garden completely with posts?"

"No," said the farmer. "We're going to cut these stalks into narrow lattes, or planks, which we'll weave in and around the posts we've already planted, using twine, when it's available, or vines to tie them off. Only then will you have a true Gabonese fence."

He chuckled at my perplexed look, clearly knowing that this was one fencing technique I had not learned in Montana!

To start us out, he grabbed one of the heavy, hollow stalks, set it on its side across the others so that one end was raised up into the air, and, with flourish, brought his machete down onto the end of the stalk. He cut into the end easily, then, with two hands, pushed on the handle and the blade on either side of the bamboo so that it cut down and into the stalk. He was splitting it. He moved the bamboo as he cut it, making sure to keep his hands away from both the sharp edge of the machete and the equally sharp edge of the newly cut bamboo.

Once he had split the stalk in two, he proceeded to split those halves again and again, until he ended up with more than a half-dozen thin-cut lattes. Grabbing—still carefully—the freshly cut bamboo, he proceeded to weave one piece through the posts on one of the sides of the garden, close to the ground. He wove one after the other, parallel to the ground and spaced about a foot above the preceding latte, growing ever higher on the posts. When he finished with the six pieces he had cut, he looked at us and said with a smile, "*À vous, mes amis*" [Now it's your turn to try, my friends]. We took turns cutting the bamboo into thin fence rails. Without the years of practice that the farmer already had, it took us much longer to cut away at the bamboo. We finally succeeded in slicing enough pieces to complete two sides, then three, then the fourth, until at long last, we had a fenced-in garden. Using twine from one of the hardware stores in town, we tied off the lattes, fastening them tightly to the posts—and to each other, at the corners—to more fully protect the precious seedling sprouts.

We even came up with our own little gate, still using the bamboo, but leaving one side untied, so it could swing in and out when needed.

While our little practice garden in the ravine on the *rive droite* did not produce baskets full of vegetables, or really much of anything beyond some beans and okra, I felt prepared to tackle a farming project once I arrived at my post in Gamba. My fencing skills had been vastly expanded upon, and if called upon to do so, I was convinced that I could construct a fence strong enough to keep out one of my family's horses—and, perhaps, even an elephant.

Peace Corps practice garden in Lambaréné

Part III: Daily Life in Gamba

My little corner of equatorial paradise is hanging in
there. This morning, I made rice pudding, and yesterday,
I baked cookies—which is interesting to do because
I don't have an oven.[11]

—JASON GRAY, LETTER TO
GRANDPARENTS, OCT. 27, 2002

Market Colors

A crowd gathered under the awning of one of the hardware stores on the main street in Gamba town. Some were looking in at the shovels, machetes, plastic buckets, hammers, and nails; others were seeking shelter from the quick, hot and heavy, early afternoon downpour. With umbrellas or plastic rain ponchos, or without, the people knew better than to brave the drenching if they could avoid it. Out in the main street, crusted potholes became soggy, filled with muddy red water, as the clay and laterite mixed together to form a potter's goo, sticking to shoes, sandals, and bike tires. And the passing taxis, which sometimes seemed to outnumber the human population in this town of seven thousand, splashed by, axles creaking as they swerved to miss the muddy puddles.

Next to the hardware store was a general supply store, with canned food items; frozen chicken (imported, bizarrely, mostly from Brazil); boxes of sugar; bags of salt; and aluminum cans and large heavy glass bottles of Fanta, Coca-Cola, and beer in the white industrial refrigerators. Many of the store owners were from West Africa (Senegal, Mali, and Morocco in particular) or from Lebanon. Customers would greet their merchant friends in French, Wolof, Bambara, Arabic, and in the universal language of hard currency—in this case, Central African francs.

This main drag, part of really the only road that looped around the town, was the central location for all things bought and sold, from electronics to food, from clothing to school books. The shipments of goods would come in sporadically, randomly, and, almost always, with mixed results. If one was waiting for a new freezer, one could wait a week or a year; it all depended on the merchant and his supply chain. One friend of mine would travel every few months to Dubai in the United Arab Emirates to bring back sophisticated cell phones and video cameras, as well as pirated movies on DVD in French and English.

Across the street from the usually foreign-owned stores stood the heart of town, the true *marché*, the market of Gamba. The market served as the central hangout, the place to see and be seen, to grab a bush-taxi ride to the next province, to greet arriving relatives and friends or wave good-bye to those departing, and to watch the other passersby…well, pass by. Wooden stalls with corrugated tin roofs were set up facing the more established stores, each operated by one or two women (for the most part), selling fresh and smoked fish from the lagoon, sweet and plantain bananas from as far away as Tchibanga, mangoes from people's backyard trees, sugarcane, manioc from the plantations around the area, and all manner of other fruits and vegetables: dull tomatoes and bright green okra, spiny pineapple, fat papaya, and peppers.

Oh, the peppers. The shades of red, bright and dark. The greens and yellows, blended with short stems and shadowed ridges. Most of the peppers were chiles, hot as habaneros, spicy, delectable, and ready to burn your tongue off.

The peppers were used in everything, from fish pepper soup to spicy, oily sauces called *piment*, placed at every restaurant table. Crush one with a spoon when you boil or sauté a chicken, then mix the sauce around in your rice. Take one bite and you exclaim, *"Ça pique, oh!"* (That stings!). Peppers have even been used to keep elephants out of plantations![12] Basically, life without spice is not really worth living. At least, that is what the pepper sellers would have you believe.

Peppers grew on short, fine bushes with emerald leaves, springing up quickly in the tropical clime, undeterred by the generally poor soil. Visiting the commercial plantation of a Nigerian friend, it was clear how important this crop was to all of the people living in Gamba. It complemented their manioc and fish, their poultry and rice, their everyday meals. My friend showed me how he carefully weeded around his pepper plants and watered them judiciously to make sure the colors were clear and bright, ready for sale. And he sold them on futures, promising his crop to the market women before they were even grown.

But back to the market. Standing next to one stall, it was easy to blend the other stalls together, with the colors of peppers and fruits, the smells of cured meats and fish, of lettuce, and, of course, many bottles of palm wine; this cornucopia was put on display beside the muddy or dusty (depending on the rains) road for all to see and purchase. I have images in my mind of the market on rainy days and sunny ones, of the bounty of the rainy season, followed by somewhat less productive days during the dry season. But always, there was something to see, some item to pick up and weigh, to smell and bargain for, speaking the constant nego-tiation of prices and importance. Whether it was a mango taken from the tree in my backyard by a neighborhood child and "repackaged" and sold by his cousin in her stall (mean-ing she had taken them from the child and now was selling them for profit as her own), or a newly brewed bottle of palm wine from an old-timer's prized palm tree, there was always something new and exciting to consider.

When I visit a farmers' market here in the United States now, I'm taken back to fond memories of picking through a not-yet-ripe bunch of plantains (500 CFA for a large bunch at the market, or about $1.00) or bartering for a better price on fresh-caught carp straight from the fisherman's impromptu "table" set up on top of his old freezer, brought up from the lagoon. And while I have the same feelings and appreciation for the love and hard work food growers and producers convey at the American weekend markets, I sometimes long for the sights and smells of the Gamba *marché*, the colors of a life in which everyone buys from the local market on a daily basis.

Making Manioc

~~~~

On the edge of the lagoon, both on the mainland and on islands, generations of Gabonese families have planted crops of peppers, mangoes, tomatoes, taro root, and manioc. Manioc, also called cassava or yuca in other parts of the world, is a hardy tuber that grows throughout the tropics. Originally from South America, *Manihot esculenta* is one of the most common sources of carbohydrates in the world. It is the base for tapioca and can be made into flour, cereal, or cooked like a potato (fried, roasted, even boiled). The tuber is covered in a hard, barky rind, which gives way to a thin layer of plant matter that contains small, cyanogenic fibers covering the starchy "meat" inside. At the tuber's core is a thick, woody cordon.

The manioc tuber grows completely underground, with a thin stalk shooting up out of the soil to four or five feet in height, and an umbrella of glossy leaves blossoming out in multiple fingers. Most families clear a small plot of land from the forest using axes, machetes, saws, and eventually fire to give space to plant their crops, and manioc quickly supplants the previous occupants once planted. With poor soil, these plots are only viable for a few years, whereupon the families will abandon the plot to create a new one further away, allowing the forest to slowly reclaim the first.

Many of these *plantations*, as they are called in Gabon, are fairly small. Around the Ndougou Lagoon, family members walk from their villages or take a boat across the lagoon to reach their plantations, sometimes daily. A principle reason for this daily trek is to try to chase away the pesky diners who come through for some free food, wreaking havoc on the family's hard work. Although the forest is full of food for the resident elephants, primates, and forest hogs, the plantations can be quite easy pickings. Other times, a plantation may simply have been placed on the path used for generations by large mammals, and they choose to walk through the plot, rather than go around. This conflict between farmers and large animals is a constant one, creating an oft tense relationship between local villagers and local wildlife. Various strategies to mitigate this conflict have included car battery or solar panel–powered electric fences, fences lined with empty cans to make noise and scare away intruding animals, or even pepper bushes planted around the perimeter of the plantation.

Once a manioc plant reaches maturity (the four- to five-foot-tall stalk with bountiful leaves), the tuber is dug out of the hard soil, often by using a machete, which is a most handy tool in the forest. To dig out a manioc tuber, one may grab the stalk above ground, then start to cut away the soil with a machete, hacking all around the tuber until one is able to pull it up by the stalk—or by hand, if one happened to cut the stalk during this endeavor. The tuber is then cleaned of dirt and set in a pile with other recently removed tubers. It is also essential to cut away and set aside the leaves, as they may be cooked with oil and fish or meat to create one of the best dishes in Gabon—*feuilles de manioc* (similar to spinach or kale, though much more flavorful).

Manioc plant

Once one has collected enough tubers, there are many ways to prepare them. All methods require the removing of the tough rind, which is possible, again, through the use of a machete (or other knife). Once the rind is removed, one must also cut away the thin layer of fibrous outer covering between the rind and the inner meat, as it is toxic. The easiest way to prepare the remaining tuber is to cut it in large chunks and fry it in palm oil or boil it like a potato. Both recipes are tasty, especially when combined with peppery fish and served with *feuilles de manioc*.

The most common method of preparing the roots in Gabon, however, is the much more labor-intensive process of creating a longer-lasting *bâton de manioc*, which is a hard, breadlike stick of cooked manioc paste. These *bâtons* keep well in the tropical humidity for several days, although the preparation process renders them devoid of most of the scant nutritional value in the original tubers. Hunters, farmers, and fishermen can bring a whole bunch of *bâtons* with them on their travels without fear of losing them to rot—and, really, without fear of anything else (animal or insect) eating them either. In the Ndougou area, residents have long made these *bâtons* quite firm, whereas people in other parts of Gabon cook them in smaller, fatter, softer packages.

Around the Ndougou Lagoon, I watched families use the *"râper/filtrer"* method to prepare *bâton de manioc*, in which one renders the tubers into a paste and then filters the paste with water before cooking. Once one has cut away the outer rind and the fibrous inner rind, one places the tubers into a bucket of water to soak for around two days. This helps soften them and settles out any remaining toxins. Then, one pounds the soaked tubers using a wooden mortar and pestle into a thick, whitish-gray paste. Next, one filters this paste with water over a sluice box–type contraption made from a wooden box with fine mesh on the bottom. Filtering the paste helps remove leftover pieces of rind and stems. Most chefs will then place the paste into an old rice sack (made from thin, woven plastic) and hang it from a branch for about a day. This process ensures that most of the water drains out, while also causing some fermentation in the heat and leaving a distinctive, sticky smell in the humid air.

Once the water has drained out and the paste has been transferred back to a large bowl, the next step is to set up a table with cleaned banana leaves. Taking two banana leaves, each with the stem of the leaf pointing in the opposite direction, one places a good quantity of manioc paste into the center and then evens it out into a straight line. Then one rolls the banana leaves widthwise, rolling them over the paste to create a *bâton* shape (like a long, thin baguette). Once the roll is complete, the stems of the leaves should still be sticking out. One folds them both into the center and wraps string or plastic ties around the newly created *bâton* to tie it off and keep it closed. When one has a number of *bâtons* finished to this point, the final step is to place them on a perforated metal grate over a hot fire to cook the manioc paste to the desired hardness. After that, they are ready for transport or to eat immediately.

Manioc takes some getting used to. I remember being served manioc during one of my first meals with my host family in Lambaréné, before learning what it was. Later, after understanding more about how it was made, how the plants grew, and how it could be served, I grew to greatly appreciate a good *bâton de manioc*. In fact, as a side to a meat or vegetable dish, soaked with good quantities of palm oil and pepper, it is hard to beat—especially once one knows how much work went in to preparing this starchy, essential dish.

Shadows on the Walls

Evening draped like curtains on the outside of the windows of my house. I enjoyed this time of the day, when the heat, although it did not completely dissipate, was brushed aside by a light breeze, whispering in the jagged palm leaves outside. This time of the day saw the noise of the nearby road subside, and the croaking of frogs and the high pitched, sonar cry of bats filled the air. Large cicada-like insects crooned from outside, occasionally silenced by a rush of wind.

Jean Pierre's family, next door, was settling in for the night. I could hear my other neighbors practicing on their drums, perhaps preparing for a funeral or wedding ceremony the coming weekend. I lived in a house situated in a group of homes owned by an extended family, which constantly saw new inhabitants. The women, some of whom were sisters, ran the show, and I got along well with the eldest sister and many of the children.

The sisters belonged to a larger, nonbiological family as well—a sisterhood in the Niembe society. They initiated women in their rituals, which included multiday healing ceremonies of drums, dance, sweating out fever, and consuming large quantities of *iboga*, that bitter, stimulating root with healing properties that my host brother Julien, the *Nganga*, had described to me in Lambaréné. In addition to being used in many secret society rites, this root is also being studied by Western doctors for its medicinal properties. It is used to stay awake on long trips through the forest and can be eaten raw, boiled in a tea, or reduced to powder form. I even heard stories of elephants going on rampages after eating too much *iboga*.

My neighbors, in addition to performing ritualistic initiation and healing ceremonies, also hired themselves out for weddings and funerals, as a way to invoke the spirits and to ensure the important cultural aspects of life were respected. The sisters were great dancers, and their husbands played the drums and sitar with gusto, usually outcompeting the electric piano from a Pentecostal church up the road or the electronic call to prayer sounding from the loudspeakers of the nearby mosque.

As I listened to the practice drums, I watched drab yellow geckos chase crane flies on the walls. And I spoke by cellular telephone to my mother back in Montana. I had never owned a cell phone before going to Gabon, but the unreliable landline infrastructure in much of Africa had been surpassed by the abundant, and more reliable, cellular infrastructure. Everyone—and, yes, their mothers—seemed to own a cell phone in Gabon!

While I described the practice drums to my mother, I kept a watch on the geckos. Gazing beyond one stalking little predator, I looked into the dark room I used as a small kitchen. The walls of my house were made of whitewashed particle board, constructed from okoumé wood. My eyes slipped passed the room, then riveted back quickly. Something was not quite right. My walls were white, but they now looked black, with strangely moving shadows.

I sprang up, still holding the phone to my ear, and stepped over to the kitchen to look at this mysterious phenomenon more closely. That's when I felt something bite my bare foot, hard. And another, and it hit me...*ants!* I told my mother that I had to go, that I would call the following week, and that I had to deal with an insect invasion.

Ants, thousands of them, coated every surface in the kitchen. The floor, the walls, the ceiling, the sink, the windows. And they were spreading out toward the rest of the house. The walls were crawling with them.

Ants like these, called army ants or driver ants, swarm through the forest in huge colonies, sometimes chased by rising waters or fire, and they sweep over everything in their path. The soldier ants have tremendous force in their mandibles, and they can devour meat in the blink of an eye. Usually, one sees thin lines of ants going to and from their colonies; however, occasionally they swarm, and many creatures much bigger than the ants will flee.

I rushed to grab my remaining bottles of insect repellant and started spraying. There were simply too many ants; the bottles ran out quickly, and aside from the little pile in front of me, I hadn't made a dent. I ran for my broom and my flip-flop sandals. The back door of the kitchen opened up onto a small stream surrounded by banana trees. I flung the door open, with ants falling from the ceiling and crawling up from the floor, biting. The creek was swollen from an earlier rain, which must have forced the ants up and into my house. I swept at them, pushing the broom through thick inches of articulated bodies, pushing them out the door. I swept at the ceiling, the walls, the floor.

Then I grabbed a pot and filled it with water, fighting off the little devils biting my arms and legs. Once the pot was nearly full, I pulled it out of the sink and flung the water onto the floor, hoping to carve a path through the ants out the door, drowning them and pushing them outside. It seemed to work. I continued to sweep the ants from the ceiling onto the floor and repeated the steps: sweep, water, sweep, slap the bugger on my leg or in my hair, sweep. After what seemed like hours of grueling work, I had succeeded in clearing the kitchen, and my home was safe. I remember thinking how lucky I was that this hadn't happened in my bedroom while I was sleeping. And I was thankful for that back door!

I swept the floor dry and went to sit back down, exhausted. The frogs kept calling, the drums were still talking, and the night had settled in to stay. Before I fell asleep, I glared at the little yellow gecko, wishing it had done a better job of protecting our home.

Nightlife

T wilight sets in early along the equator. With roughly twelve hours of daylight, starting around 6:00 a.m., the darkness descends at 6:00 p.m. (or 18h00 in Gabon) and fully blankets everything by 7:00 p.m. After a busy day of work, play, study, or even a not-so-busy day, the quotidian question arises: what to do tonight? In a place like Gamba, even though it is quite small, there are actually many options for nightlife, from restaurants to dancing, from sports to cultural ceremonies, to outdoor adventures. It all depends on the season, how one feels, and whom one knows.

A visit to the Ibonga turtle camp on the beach is an amazingly rewarding late-night outing. Assisting the turtle researchers in their nightly study can yield peaceful strolls along pristine beaches, enjoying the cool night breeze while participating in measuring an enormous female leatherback turtle laying her eggs.

Or, as has happened to me, one can spend the evening defending one's home from an invasion of angry, biting insects.

In Gamba, my favorite nighttime activity was to sit with friends over a late dinner under the stars (assuming it was not raining). Gamba boasts many small barbeque restaurants, such as Le Perroquet or Au Bambou, where tables and chairs are set up on the sandy ground and the chefs bring out braised chicken or grilled barracuda brochettes, with fried rice and tomato sauce and garnished with spicy *piment* peppers, mayonnaise, and Dijon-style mustard. As is true anywhere, sharing such a meal with a date, or simply with friends and family, is always special.

For me, these simple dishes under a diamond-studded sky, which seemed close enough to touch, were somehow more; enjoying a conversation with Bas Huijbregts, the then–program manager of WWF Gamba, discussing various research projects and financing efforts, tactics on protecting wildlife, or discussing local culture with our local colleagues…those nights stand out in my mind.

And, ever important for such conversations and meals was partaking in the time-honored ceremony of sipping on a bottle or two of Gabonese beer—usually the national beer, Régab. Bas and I once sat at the Bambou, drinking and talking as a blazing lightning storm lit up over the lagoon. Electricity arced across the sky like fireworks, up and down, sideways.

After finishing up at one of these grill joints, Bas and I would move off to one of the many small bars around town. These bars were usually managed by Congolese or Cameroonian women. Although I never conducted a formal survey, my sense is that Gamba has one of the highest per-capita bar-to-person ratios in all of Gabon. One cannot travel more than a few hundred yards around the single main road in town without coming across a little wooden stall with tables and chairs set up outside and a loud stereo blaring out Congolese or Ivoirian dance music.

In any case, after a plate of barbequed chicken or fried whole fish, it was pleasant to head down the street to enjoy another beer and to gain a different vantage point for further people-watching. And in such a small town, it was easy to get to know not only the bartenders but also the other patrons.

Occasionally, these late dinners would be followed by a trip to one of two local dance clubs. Imagine another wooden structure, with room enough for twenty people, with a bar inside and a loud stereo system and disco-ball lights. Then add in another thirty to fifty people, and you'll get a good picture of a Gabonese night club. The two clubs I occasionally attended were the Crépuscule (meaning "dusk" in French) and the Greenpeace. Like the bars around town, these two clubs were right next to each other in the market. Every night of the week, the clubs would be packed with people out for a good time. Still, I much preferred hours of conversation with Bas or other friends to the sweaty dance clubs.

Another excellent nighttime activity, if one was lucky enough to be invited, was to attend a traditional ceremony like a funeral or a wedding. Families would hire out a troupe of traditional dancers, singers, and drummers like my neighbors, who would dress up in raffia and white cloth, paint their faces white, and dance as if possessed by some other force around a roaring fire, to the beat of one or more talking drums. I attended a fair number of my neighbors' performances, which could last for more than twenty-four hours, while the actual ceremonies could go on for days.

On other nights, I headed down to an open-air, but roofed, community center and sports complex constructed by Shell Gabon. This facility was endowed with a basketball court, an old Ping-Pong table, and even a small gym. Large festivals and fairs were frequently held in this facility, and musical events, such as the fabulous Gabonese singer Annie-Flore Batchiellilys, would perform from time to time. I spent many nights competing with my friends around that Ping-Pong table. In fact, my Nigerian friend, who grew peppers to sell at the Gamba *marché,* was one of the best players around.

But none of the Gamba nightlife compares to an evening in Setté Cama.

With less than ninety permanent residents, it still amazes me how much one could do at night in Setté Cama village. From catching forest crabs on the beach, to accompanying Jean Pierre in a pirogue to impress and astound visiting friends or family by hand-catching young crocodiles hiding in the mangrove roots (one could see where they were hiding by the reflected flashlight beam in their golden, reptilian eyes), to sitting on the beach and being serenaded by the crashing waves, Setté Cama has this dreamlike, paradise quality to it. I remember taking nighttime walks through the forest paths, feeling tense for fear of encountering an elephant, and listening for chimpanzees, enjoying the call of a frog, or seeing sparkling spider eyes when I shone my flashlight into the moist, sparse grasses.

I remember sitting around the fire with village elders and their families, sipping palm wine and feebly attempting to communicate in Yilumbu, causing everyone to burst out laughing at my pronunciation or word choice. And I remember sharing fish soup with Jean Pierre and his family, his wife Angélique and his boys, Dan and Dylan.

After dinner, Jean Pierre would start up the small village generator and rev up his bar/dancehall, Kam Doli, which inevitably brought the entire village, including any tourists and wildlife officials stationed at the entrance to Loango National Park, for a night of dancing, libations, and good times. Kam Doli, to this day, is my favorite "club," perhaps because I helped in the construction and outfitting of it (a strobe light and miniature disco ball I gave to Jean Pierre are apparently still there); more likely, though, I love its location underneath a massive mango tree on the edge of the Ndougou Lagoon, and the simple fact that it is the hangout for the entire village.

My memories of this diverse nightlife are blended, mixed, and jumbled. I also spent many nights simply relaxing, low-key and quiet. But when the need arose to dance or listen to loud music, or to grab a meal and relax with a friend, Gamba, Setté Cama, and, really, much of Gabon, never failed to disappoint.

Baobab and Brochettes

⌇

They say that tastes and smells are extremely important for memory, that our most intense recollections are triggered by odors and flavors.[13] I can attest to this; sometimes a random scent seems to bring me completely back to a conversation or action that occurred in a restaurant or at a friend's home, or a delectable meal melts into my receptive tongue and I am reminded of something or someone. So what better way to share a glimpse into life in Gabon than to include a few thoughts and memories of favorite restaurants in Gamba?

Some of the best meals in Gamba are at an eatery right off of the central market, at a place called the Baobab. The Baobab is owned by the Sow family from Senegal. Abou Sow, the patriarch, has a small compound of rooms and buildings, including a hardware store, impromptu electronics sales (from the hardware store), family rooms, and the restaurant. One of his nephews, Diabel Sow, is known to the entire town, as his friendly nature, generosity, and capacity to laugh are legendary. Diabel also ran the hardware store while I was living in Gamba, and he was always up for a weekend at the beach or a night out on the town—especially at the Greenpeace dance club.

The actual restaurant was operated by Madame Dia (pronounced "Ja"), an extraordinary chef, who somehow seemed to know all of her customers and their families, even if she had only just met them. Madame Dia brought to life the tastes and smells of ginger and garlic, of hibiscus and soursop, making wonderful frozen drinks from hibiscus leaves (called *bissap*); yogurt (sour milk) drinks, using the fleshy soursop fruit (called *karasol* in French) from a tree in the Sow compound; and a potent liquid remedy for colds and common ailments, made from the spiciest ginger root around.

The Baobab is famous for its lamb and chicken dishes, which are common in many Muslim restaurants, but Madame Dia rendered a leg of lamb or a breast of chicken so smooth that the meat would melt off the bone, tingling down your throat with pepper spice and caramelized onions. It is even more renowned for the signature Senegalese dish, the *thiebou djenn* (pronounced "cheboo jen"). This amazing dish is made from braised fish, fresh from the lagoon, with a tomato, okra, garlic, salt, and spicy chile pepper sauce, set on top of fried rice sautéed in palm oil and tomato sauce. A simple dish, my simple description does not do it justice; I must have eaten hundreds of pounds of *thiebou djenn* during my three years in Gabon. All of these meals were made rich and thick partly because of the fresh palm oil in which they were cooked, as palm oil is one of the major products made in the country.

While the meals at the Baobab were superb and inexpensive, my favorite time with the Sow and Dia families was spent in the kitchen, in the family living room, and in the small courtyard behind the restaurant. Huge skillets and bowls of food, the same used in the actual restaurant, were presented to the large family (including cousins, friends, and neighbors, as a Senegalese family is not limited to blood relations) and doled out in huge portions onto metal plates, from which each person ate with his or her hands, not with utensils, and shared personal stories and news with everyone present.

The best meals were those immediately after the breaking of the holy month of Ramadan (called the *carême* in Gabon), which usually involved a whole lamb, purchased and transported by *taxi-brousse* from Tchibanga, well fed during the holy month, then bled, braised, grilled, and rendered delicious for a huge celebration of life and faith and friends and family. These feasts were unbeatable, and Madame Dia outdid herself each time.

Following these amazing meals, or even just during various parts of the day, Diabel would prepare the traditional offering of mint tea (called *Ataï*), combined with just the right amount of caramelized sugar, mint leaves, and boiled gunpowder green tea leaves. The tea was served piping hot in small shot glasses, on which Diabel worked his presentation magic by cooling the glasses with cool water, swirling a small amount of hot tea around to create a foam of bubbles, and then pouring from the tea pot by holding it about two feet above the tiny glasses for a perfect stream of dark, sweet, potent tea cascading into the glass. Depending on the number of people, the normal way of drinking was to sip slowly, and then repeat the process two more times.

I used to sit on bags of cement in the hardware store chatting with other customers and sharing in this drink, or reposing on a small stool under an unused market stall as a visiting Sow relative or the local imam dispensed wisdom to the younger folks as we shared the tea. It made no matter who in the group was Muslim or not, the wisdom usually dealt with relationships and life, not directly with faith. And these tea ceremonies were even conducted at the beach, in between volleyball games. Today, when I drink Moroccan mint tea or try to make my own, à la Diabel, every small glass reminds me of some conversation shared with friends in Gamba.

My memories of Gabon are not limited to Senegalese food, of course. One of the best Gabonese restaurants in Gamba is Le Perroquet, which means "The Parrot." This little spot is hidden back in a small neighborhood, adjacent to an empty field (at least it was when I was there). Loga, the owner and chef, is friendly and smiling, never afraid to make a joke at her customers' or her own expense. She is the master of grilling fish, shrimp, and meat on a set of charcoal barbeques situated near the tables set up outside the small bar in the restaurant. Large freshwater prawns (called "*gambas*") caught around the lagoon are braised to perfection with oil, chile pepper, garlic, and mayonnaise. These thick, orange crustaceans are then skewered and grilled, before Loga brings them out, piping hot, served next to a huge mound of fried red (from the palm oil) rice or accompanied by manioc or fried plantains. A thick breast and leg of chicken, or braised carp or snapper, succulent and flaky, can substitute for the skewered prawns.

But my absolute favorite meal at Le Perroquet was the brochettes of barracuda. Loga takes a massive fillet of barracuda, caught that same day in the Ndougou, and cuts it into thick, square chunks, which are then placed on the skewer, braised, and grilled. Served with any side dish, these brochettes are absolutely amazing!

Bas Huijbregts and Jean Pierre at lunch with colleagues at Le Perroquet

My mouth is watering as I write this, remembering how the smoke from the grill wafts over onto the waiting diners, a smoky, gamy smell of barbequed fish steaks and spicy peppers, of grilled and fried onions, and tomato sauce. When you sit down at Le Perroquet, you can relax with a Régab *bien glacée* (well chilled), the national beer of Gabon, served in a 750 ml bottle, while you chat with friends or with Loga (an inevitable occurrence) and listen to your stomach rumble as the smells and sounds of cooking fish reach out and tease your nose and mouth.

Rain on the Roof

The heat hung heavy as twilight overtook the long day, like someone had pulled down a shade over the sinking sun. Temperature played off of the nearly 100 percent humidity, making breathing, moving, and even thinking lugubrious, difficult, and sweaty. "Like swimming through molasses," was one expression I had heard used, though come to think of it, I have never known of anyone to actually swim through molasses.

When the air sizzles in the evening, hot and dripping, it usually means that something has to give; some invisible switch is pulled somewhere to release the heat that rises from the ground, seeking an escape. And often, the trigger may take the form of low, roiling black clouds, electric charges, and lightening, opening up the sky so the heat vents out. As the hot air rises, freed from its earthly coils, it pulls apart those clouds just enough so that it leaves behind its dripping humidity, which combines with whatever moisture is holed up in the rumbling storm and forms monstrous drops. Each drop seems to pull at other drops, until—and one can literally feel that instant right before it happens—they all start to fall, inexorably, inevitably, and more heavily than the fleeing heat.

At that moment, the air cools quickly, as if in anticipation of the gravity-induced deluge that is about to come. And come down it does, hard.

As I sat one evening beneath the corrugated metal roof of my house, the hairs on my arms and the back of my neck felt the electricity in the air caused by the rising, fading heat, and my muscles tensed, then relaxed the moment the *chaleur* (heat) broke. Then my ears picked up the slightest *tac, tac, tac* as the first sprinkles formed, before the roaring whoosh and constant drumming that followed. On a night like this, the electricity would often go out, as power lines were shocked by water, or perhaps someone shut it down to avoid any accidents (since the lines were often jerry-rigged and sometimes hung low over the ground). Whatever the case, I loved lighting a candle in the noisy dark, watching the flame flicker and twirl, dancing around like a drunken reveler, as the rain fell with such a force as to create its own wind.

It is hard to describe the sound of this much water on a metal roof. It is loud enough in the forest, crashing through leaves and branches, puddling up and eventually flooding out the ground cover. It is noisy when you sit in your tent, huddled and cold, hoping the tent can withstand the pounding, and hoping the ground wasn't wet enough already to result in a large pool flooding you out. Under a metal roof, however, it feels like you are in a wind tunnel, with a massive fan blowing water all around you. Like a million crashing waves, landing continuously on top of your home, rendering discussions, reading, any activity other than primal meditation on the nature of life nearly impossible.

This phenomenon can—and does—happen at any time of day. It certainly makes teaching class (or learning) a challenge. But it is possible to get used to it, in some fashion. My Gabonese friends take it as an inevitable fact of life, this downpour, this torrent of water and sound. People will calmly wait it out or accept the fact that they are going to get wet, so might as well just slog through it. A dinner party or evening at home might be extended with simple shrugs, as if to say, "Here we go again." I also began to take it in stride, although waking from a deep sleep because of a deafening thunderclap or lightening crack or from the roar on the roof, is definitely an unforgettable experience. And whatever they said, I know my friends were surprised sometimes too by the ferocity of these deluges.

On this particular night, as the heat left and the rain came, I enjoyed the cooling of the air, the rush of pounding water, and being inside, out of the rain. My candle flickered happily, as if it too knew that only inside would it find shelter and safety tonight.

And as quickly as it came, the rain let up, from a constant hammer to a light rapping, to an occasional patter, then nothing. And the world took a collective breath, before releasing its normal evening sounds into the now-cleaned air. These rains could last for minutes or hours, each time releasing the heat and returning some measure of coolness.

Behind my house, after every rain event, a fast-flowing stream would form, occasionally flooding in through my back door. This stream had the soothing sound common to such bodies of flowing water, and it fed a symphony of frogs and cicadas, crickets and hooting owls. This same stream also brought the occasional serpent, bedraggled chicken, and insect infestation to my doorstep. Once the frogs started croaking and crooning, the other night sounds would finally brave their way out from their hiding places, so that I could hear the soft barking cough of a gecko, the scratching, digging sounds of a chicken excavating for insects brought to the surface by the rain, and the filtered noise from my neighbors and the street one hundred yards up from the path to my house. Like some scripted musical, life always started moving again after its short repose from the rains.

Sitting on my rattan couch, watching the dancing flame of the now-shortened candle, I smiled as the noises, the calls and laughter, the cries of babies and insects washed over me in much gentler fashion than the storm. I relished the thought of the next hot, sweltering, unbearably sweaty day, because the heat must be released; and when it was, that silent, suspended moment of cool before the downpour, followed by the reawakened senses after the storm, is magical.

As my candle went out, tired from its struggle to bring light to the dark room, I fell asleep with a smile, dreaming of rain and metal roofs.

Part IV: Conservation Beginnings

We owe it to ourselves and to the next generation to conserve the environment so that we can bequeath our children a sustainable world that benefits all.

—WANGARI MAATHAI

Conservation Photography, Eye in the Sky

We banked left, hovering over the water like a pied kingfisher, slowly rounding the turn before straightening the nose. A tattooed baboon adorned the tail fin, sitting zenlike—Rafiki from the *Lion King*. The engine purred loudly, rumbling with seemingly unnatural force as it carried us up and over the water. This little two-seater Cessna 182 was flown by a pilot from the Wildlife Conservation Society and was aiding a team of Smithsonian Institution photographers to capture images from the sky—a bird's eye view of the lagoon, the forest, the place—images of the health of the forest. This painted metal eagle soared out of the little Gamba airport and above the multicolored landscape of Gabon.

The plane was outfitted with two seats, and the rear storage area immediately behind the seats had been cleared out. In this empty space, the principal Smithsonian photographer,

Carlton Ward, Jr., loaded all of his gear. Then the rear door was removed to give unfettered room for quick repositioning of long and short lenses. On this particular day, I had been invited to tag along.

Shortly after liftoff, we edged out over the Ndougou Lagoon. I sat behind Carlton, looking out the window opposite the open door. He must have brought along five or six cameras, and he shot both digital and film, using multiple-sized lenses as he switched from one camera to the next. The water seemed to slip away and solidify into a short strip of foliage, which then abruptly fell off into a tawny coastal savannah. Near the interface of grasses and forest, a reddish streak ran by. A small herd of forest buffalo ran from the shadow of the plane. Carlton snapped several shots of these ungulates. His photos would help document any illegal logging, aiding researchers and conservationists in their management efforts to preserve this remarkable forest and its wildlife.

The plane leveled out and headed north, back over the lagoon and up toward isolated Lac Divangui. We followed the muddy Rembo Bongo River through its snaking turns, sometimes losing it where the dense canopy was thickest. The glossy leaf clusters of greens, reds, and yellows seemed to jump up toward us from the ground, capturing the eye and creating a natural-oiled canvas of rainbow hues. Leaves blended into flower blossoms on a neighboring tree, seeming to light up as we glided overhead.

We turned north and west, leaving the river; and eventually, a dark mirror, reflecting the cloudy sky, appeared amid the trees. The lake spidered out from the forest into many small streams, like a giant amoeba. The pilot swooped lower, until we were only a few hundred feet above the multicolored canopy. The water of the lake was tinged with tannins and mud. And as we passed over, from the corner of my eye, I saw a grayish shape rise up from the depths and then quickly dive, ripples spreading out. I believe I caught a glimpse of an endangered West African manatee, surprised by the small plane flying over its normally secluded refuge.

The fleeting vision of aquatic animal was brief enough, and perhaps imagined enough, that no one else on the flight saw it—there were no pictures taken of my manatee (or whatever else it may have been). But it did not matter. The plane had flown on, and we were pointed west, over the forest. An occasional burst of orange leaves jutted out of the green sea below, bubbling up from single trees like giant, leafy cotton candy. Birds flew over the trees, gliding below and sometimes disappearing back into the dark green subcanopy. The roar of the Cessna's engine blanketed out all other sounds, but I could imagine the birds' calls, the wind in the branches, and the many hoots and screams of guenon monkeys.

As we went further west, edging toward the ocean, a curious bunch of smoky clouds rose from the forest. From a distance, these dark gray plumes gave the impression of individual trees, spaced far apart from each other, lit like huge candles. Then the plane swung toward one plume, and I realized it was an oil well head, with a smoke stack reaching above the canopy, flaring off natural gas released during the drilling process. The gas was burned, flaming and smoking high into the air. There were other stacks jutting up through the forest, throwing fire and smoke up to the winds. We had entered the air space of the onshore Rabi-Kounga oil field operation, which had been producing crude oil for Shell Gabon for the last two decades. Many of the inhabitants of Gamba town worked these fields, and this was the first time I had seen them from the air. On later flights between Gamba and Libreville, especially at night, it was possible to see the fires above the canopy, spread out like fireflies. We turned back toward Gamba after reaching this oil field partially hidden in the trees.

Seated on the floor of the storage compartment, I was able to watch not only the forest below, but also a masterful photographer plying his trade. Carlton later published a book with the Smithsonian Institution, *The Edge of Africa* (Hylas Publishing, 2003), which includes some of the photos taken during that flight. His pictures show an intact forest and strong populations of multiple species. They also show the dangers of overlogging, the impact of oil pipelines and roads on the forest, and highlight many of the fascinating people of the lagoon.

Carlton maneuvered around the tight space, switching from one camera to the next, leaning nearly outside of the open cargo door to capture the color, the mystery, and the majesty of the forest. Once he'd had his fill, he put his cameras, lenses, film, and other gear back into their cases, and yelled out to me through the headphones, above the noise of the engine, to see if I wanted to take his place by the opening to snap some of my own photos. I happily moved over and felt the rush of the wind outside. He motioned to me to make sure my camera and lens never protruded out of the plane, as they would be ripped away by the wind. We did not see any more animals, but I did take plenty of pictures of the canopy, of individual trees and landscapes. I remember the feeling of leaning toward the opening as the plane would bank left, giving me an unobstructed view straight down into the forest, allowing me to pretend for a moment that I, too, was a master photographer.

I quickly snapped a couple rolls of film as the plane edged back toward the Gamba airport. The last half hour of the flight was delightful, as I set my camera down and simply gazed out of the opening into the vast forest below. Then, before the plane glided over the lagoon and away from the forest, I snapped one last mental photograph of the colors and shapes of individual trees as they blended together into an impressionistic whole.

Gabon village as seen from above

Rosy Bee-Eaters

Early one morning during my first year in Gabon, a small group of us set out from our camp on the coastal plain, set back several hundred yards from the beach. Green tents rose like large ant hills situated about ten feet from each other, some contained dark shapes just beginning to stir. This was a Smithsonian Institution research camp, full of botanists, ecologists, zoologists, camp cooks, research assistants, and a few guests. The goal of this camp was to survey the biodiversity of a small portion of Loango National Park over the course of roughly two months, documenting species numbers, threats to habitat, and ecologically sensitive areas within the park.

The camp lay a full day's walk from the outlet of the lagoon to the south, roughly a third of the way up into the park. I had walked in the day before, passing more than thirty forest buffalo and about twenty elephants, some of which blocked the passage for long minutes. I had been granted permission by park authorities and the Smithsonian to walk up and spend a couple of nights with the researchers, and I led a conservation tourist (and eventual Smithsonian employee) and a WWF volunteer to the camp. We had arrived late at night, just ahead of the high tide, and I had signed us up for an early morning field trek.

As the dawn lay in wait above the canopy to the east, we followed several bird researchers, including one from Panama, one from Cameroon, and one from Gabon. I tagged along with my binoculars and camera, thrilled at the chance to follow these professional birders as they sought to understand and document the avian life in Loango. The researchers carried a large microphone to record bird calls and songs, as the many species woke and started their day. They had such an impressive knowledge of the bird calls; they would hear a quick chirp or a soft whistle and name the species without a moment's hesitation. I tried to cock my head to one side to better catch these fleeting sounds, but I knew it would take me years to come to recognize even a fraction of the song bank these professionals had at their disposal. Although it is extremely exciting to actually see the singers, recording songs in the forest is a much quicker, surer way of counting species than visual observations, given the ease with which the roughly 450 documented species in Loango National Park are able to blend into the forest.

After following the ornithologists for roughly an hour, we left the trees and entered an open, sandy clearing, with sharp grass growing in clumps from the white sand. Following their lead, I watched the forest edge, hoping for a glimpse of a warbler, or even a parrot. We heard the loud call of a distant hornbill and saw a small flock of African Grey Parrots rise from the top of an ozouga tree. The morning light was still dim, and the microphone recording was still more accurate than our eyes.

The Gabonese researcher, Martin Ombenentori, told us about another part of the clearing, where he guaranteed that we would see some stunning birds. He explained where to go but did not tell us what we would see. At the edge of the clearing, maybe ten feet from the forest, sat a small tarp jutting out of the ground, covered by dried leaves and branches, propped up by several more branches. It was a hide—specifically, a photographer's hide, set up previously by Carlton Ward, Jr., the Smithsonian photographer. We climbed in and settled down onto the sand with cameras ready.

A few minutes later, I saw something—a sharp, needle-curved beak, jutting out from a dark head and back, with a bright white stripe under the eye, and a brilliant rosy breast. Dozens of dark heads peeked up from the white sandy clearing, hidden at first by the sparse grasses; then whole bodies appeared, as the birds emerged from their subterranean nests, stretching and preening in the early morning light. We sat in the small, covered hide, hidden by the dry leaves and branches, watching the sand and these magnificent rosy bee-eaters. They took flight in waves, arcing up into the morning air above the clearing, catching insects that were just entering the warming air. The birds would sit, quietly watching the skies above the clearing, surrounded by dark forest. The morning light, although dimmed by clouds, started to reflect off of the brilliant rose-colored feathers, drawing my eyes to one, then another, as they emerged, stretched, then jumped into flight, disappearing into the skies, only to swoop back down and land right in front of us.

More birds continued to pop up out of the ground, where they had dug small nest cavities in which to sleep and hide. They reminded me somewhat of similar colonies in my home state of Montana, where prairie dogs construct massive networks of tunnels and underground rooms. The bee-eaters did not construct tunnels, but they were equally adept at going under and disappearing, then reappearing en masse as the morning insect hunt commenced. It is amazing that these birds are able to dig into the sand, lacking arms, hands, fingers. Instead, they use their sharp beaks like chisels; then they kick the loose sand away, until they are finally able to nest in these labor-intensive holes.

Rosy bee-eaters in Loango National Park

I took a few photographs, but for the most part, I sat back and watched. It was an amazing experience, just to observe these communal birds, hidden under the earth by night, flashing their bright rosy underbellies by day, sweeping up and down to the symphony of morning light and the awakening forest around them. I remember wondering how safe the ground nesting was, and I am not sure whether they post sentries at night or simply rely on their numbers for the colony's survival. In any case, these brave, beautiful birds still take flight in my mind's eye, emerging from the darkness of forgetfulness into the slow dawn with renewed energy, swooping flight, and gorgeous, rose-colored feathers.

Wading in the Swamp

Pick up one foot carefully, pulling it out of the vacuum of mud as the other sinks in. Step out, careful to test the ground for trip-wire roots, buried logs, or other things unseen, and settle your weight down and forward onto your newly placed foot, while the other tries to escape the quicksandlike soil. One after the other, slow step by slow step, goes a loose line of backpack-wearing explorers. You take a look around as each leg labors through the mud and water. Trees, stunted and drowned, struggle up toward the obscured sky of gray. Some monstrous trunks seem to fade into the background as the thin, newer growth fingers up out of the wet swamp.

And then you remember where you are, belly deep in dark, reddish water, struggling to keep most of your backpack as dry as possible, while each foot stumbles and strikes out at a maze of oozing mud and sharp, sunken branches. Bubbles occasionally erupt behind with a sickly sweet smell of sulfur, like eggs left out too long on the counter. Were those gases released from the mud as you picked up your foot, or were the bubbles caused by some unseen creature, slithering around you under the water? You look ahead to the line leader, pushing his way through the wet, wading north and east, trying to follow a straight line. *Is that an eye poking up behind him, blinking?* you wonder. Pythons live in these parts, as do dwarf crocodiles and slender-snouted crocodiles and (this is what you are really thinking) Nile crocodiles. Step by step, follow the leader....

The Smithsonian Institution had been conducting biological inventories around the Ndougou Lagoon, assessing faunal and floral diversity, habitat types, and generally determining what was out there. This research involved long days, weeks, even months of walking transect lines and live-trap lines, inspecting both mist nets and bucket traps, and traipsing through the forest and water with low-tech and high-tech monitoring equipment. Researchers from around the world were flown in to assess the biodiversity and eco-system health of the Ndougou region, including in Loango and Moukalaba-Doudou National Parks. Their findings were critical to determine how best to manage and protect the national parks and wildlife which live within them. However, before the researchers could come, permanent staff and local employees were tasked with determining where the researchers could set up the base camps, from which they would venture out daily (and nightly) to conduct their surveys.

I was invited on one of these exploratory expeditions by Michelle Lee, the field program manager for the Smithsonian

Institution in Gabon. Michelle had been working in Gamba for several years before I arrived and had become a good friend. She and her staff assisted Jean Pierre and me with education activities in schools around the lagoon.

Our goal for this expedition was to find a suitable location for a rotating team of dozens of researchers and support staff to camp for several months in the foothills of the Doudou Mountains of Moukalaba-Doudou National Park. These mountains, the tallest of which is one thousand meters high, rise up from the dense forests northeast of the Ndougou Lagoon. To reach them, one has to hike in from the east side, a trip of many days, or take a boat from Gamba town, either up the Rembo Bongo (sometimes called the N'Dogo River) and hike in from the west, or hike north from the shore of the lagoon.

Michelle's team consisted of friends of mine who worked for the Smithsonian Institution, most of whom had grown up in villages around the lagoon. We first went up the river, passing through papyrus fields of puffy green heads on tall stems. The river wound its way south from the mountains, draining the vast forest and feeding the Ndougou Lagoon. A swift current pulled at the boat, trying to force us back down the river, but our motor stuck the course and we gradually left the papyrus and the lagoon behind and entered a humid tunnel of green canopy. An osprey cried behind us, presumably spotting its meal in the no-longer-visible lagoon. Black tsetse flies, attracted by dark clothing, would land on our clothes and packs, looking for a meal. When an occasional wind picked up, or the boat sped north at a sufficient speed, the flies could not catch us. But from time to time, they would strike—hard, like a horsefly.

The Rembo Bongo is a very narrow river, no more than fifty feet wide in some places; and in other areas, depending on the rains, it became impassible for a motor boat. It also fed into a series of deep-forest lakes, hidden from the world by lowland forest. Fishing villages and camps are situated along its banks, and we passed several pirogues laden with nets, elderly men, and young children. Most of the fishermen were known to us, and we to them, as the lagoon eventually brought everyone together in Gamba town. The river banks were soggy mud tracks, making it nearly impossible to pull the boat out of the current or to unload our gear.

From time to time, downed logs from fallen trees stuck out from all directions, requiring us to pull in the motor and paddle or, in shallow spots, to get out and pull the boat around a sandbank. These logs also dotted the edge of the water, leaning down and disappearing like dark, woody slides. Egrets and African darters would perch on the logs, craning their long, slender necks to spear unsuspecting fish. Dark blue giant kingfishers, with black beaks and russet breasts, glided low over the water to land on a branch, watching us pass by.

And some logs hid other denizens of the watery domain—a low, long, slender-snouted crocodile nearly camouflaged perfectly. Its lengthy snout was a suitable weapon to snatch a fish or frog underwater, while its six-foot-long body and powerful tail could propel it silently away from our boat, slipping into the water and disappearing.

All of this entranced me: Michelle and the others pointed out what was most likely a putty-nosed monkey crossing above us through the canopy. I spotted a Malachite kingfisher silently spying on our progress from a dead branch hanging low over the water. This bird was brilliant blue and orange and not nearly as large as its dark blue cousin.

We set up our first camp in one of the few actual clearings on the shoreline, with a small sandbar leading up to a hill of short grasses and old termite mounds in the shape of enormous mushrooms. As soon as the boat stopped, the tsetse flies came back, but we shrugged out of our dark packs and set them off to the side as we cleared some space for our tents. Since it was still not yet midday, our plan was to hike out to the east, in the hopes of determining whether we could establish a relatively easy route into the Doudou Mountains. The expedition was designed to find as easy an access as possible to bring in supplies, people, and research equipment.

We started out by following the compass east. The forest was thin near the clearing but quickly began to grow denser. The land was flat for perhaps a mile, before beginning to dip and rise into the foothills leading to the mountains. Yet these hills proved steep—and muddy. And after several hours, it was decided that this would not be the best choice of routes for setting up a several-months base camp for research activity. So we hiked back to the river, scrambling up and down sloppy slopes and grabbing onto branches to halt the occasional fall.

Once we reached the campsite, it was nearing suppertime. I helped gather up some of the old, now-empty termite mounds in the clearing after one of the team members explained that when burned, they released a natural insecticide. He believed that this was caused by the chemical secretions the termites used to hold their homes together. In any case, once our tents were set up and the fire was lit, the light started to fade, and the tsetse flies disappeared. We ate a meal of canned cassoulet along with rice and manioc. After supper, with twilight in full force, the mosquitoes came in to attack. But we were ready and threw some of the now-crushed termite mounds into the fire. They caught fire and smoked, blanketing us in a not-unpleasant scent that seemed to keep the majority of the mosquitoes away from our skin. But to be safe, we all retreated to our tents and curled up in our bedsheets to get some sleep.

Early the next morning, after some Nescafé and bread, we loaded our gear into the boat and motored up the river. We tried a couple of small tributaries that led into the foothills, but the water became shallow, and boat passage was completely blocked. We ended up heading back down the river, speeding along with the current and startling several slender-snouted crocodiles before passing the papyrus fields and reentering the lagoon.

After consulting the maps and observing the banks of the lagoon and the time of day, we decided to try a different tactic. We turned the boat toward the northeasternmost portion of the lagoon and pulled onto the muddy shore through small, thin saplings and tied the boat to one of them. We would try to hike north into the foothills.

The ground was wet, ankle-deep at first, and muddy. Yet, we were all in good spirits. It was still morning and the sense of adventure, of scouting a course for the substantial amount of conservation research that was to come, was exciting. We talked softly as we walked, pointing out where the trees seemed more sparse, perhaps where it would be easiest to bring equipment through. The ankle-high water slowly faded away, until our feet hit drier (though still muddy) ground. But this "dry" spot was short-lived. Our boots were quickly resubmerged in dark water. And then it got deeper, knee high…waist high…eventually, chest high for a brief time.

I held my pack up to keep it dry, to keep my tent and food out of the dark water. And our soft discussions became a memory, as each of us struggled to find our footing, and we spread out into a line in the hopes of again regaining drier ground.

Slowly, our compass bearing was thrown off kilter, as the hours dragged on without finding higher ground. It was difficult to keep a straight line when unseen roots and snags bar your way in waist-to-chest-deep water. Each step leads you slightly off your path as you maneuver around underwater obstacles. And your mind plays tricks on you, with the bubbling smells and the knowledge that there are crocodiles in this part of the world.

Despite those nagging fears, we couldn't help but notice that the snarls and saplings that seemed to thrive in this swamp sprouted leaves of incredible shapes, sizes, and colors. Greens and yellows, round and oblong, reds and browns and whites, all somehow reflected in the dank, ochre and rust-colored water. An occasional sunbeam would pierce the canopy and shoot through the leafy rainbow to create a Chihuly-esque scene all around us.

Eventually, we found some higher ground after what seemed like days of trudging through the mud, and we stopped to eat some canned Spam-like meat and manioc, hands drenched in sweat and mud, and smelling somewhat of sulfur. The "dry" land helped make this meal a feast. While we ate, we discovered some monstrous leeches stuck to our stomachs and legs, having somehow oozed their way under our clothes. Carefully, I grabbed these four-inch slimy annelids one by one and pulled them from my body. They were so swollen with blood that they came away easily, and I flung them back into their watery abode. We quickly decided to turn back; this route was no easier than the steep hill climb the day before.

Back to the boat we trudged, edging our way one foot after another, grumbling about the wet and heat. The boat, thankfully still tied to its small tree, took us home to Gamba town. Although our scouting had failed to find the right path, from a conservation and planning perspective, the excursion was worthwhile; it provided important reconnaissance of the terrain, some of the local biodiversity, and a good idea of where *not* to set up a base camp.

Michelle's team made one more trip into the swamp shortly thereafter and found a shorter route to higher, drier land. It turns out our hours-long trek through waist-high murk had skirted the high ground by a few hundred yards. The Smithsonian was able to clear a small water path through the swampiest parts of the forest and brought people and gear in by pirogue to the high ground, where they built a small dock, created a trail up into the foothills, and set up a world-class base camp, equipped with a photo studio, kitchen, and platforms to keep tents, clothing, equipment, and researchers as dry as possible in the wet forests of the Moukalaba-Doudou National Park.

I later spent some time trailing researchers on botanical surveys and nighttime chameleon hunts at the camp in the Doudou Mountains, helping to inventory the area's biological resources and prepare a management plan for the national park. What remains strongest in my mind to this day about that trek through the swamp are the colors of the leaves we encountered while wading up to our chests in muddy waters, as well as the hope that eventual research would aid in conserving this part of Gabon.

Gorilla's Hand

Moukalaba-Doudou. The very name sounds like a fictitious place, some dreamed-up landscape deep in the heart of a forgotten jungle. In fact, it stands for an impressive and, based on my prior swamp-wading experience, sometimes inaccessible national park northeast of the Ndougou Lagoon. From the flat, coastal plain and lowland forest, foothills rise up like the shrugged shoulders of a waking giant. These hills transform into the Monts Doudou, with an elevation of 1,000 meters. These mountains rise from sea level to their full height, but are not peaked. Instead, they are rounded, covered in trees, and nowhere offer the views typical of rocky peaks. Still, they act to capture rainwater and pool it in this portion of the Congo Basin, where it empties into lagoons, rivers, and lakes, eventually draining into the Atlantic Ocean.

On the far eastern side of Moukalaba-Doudou National Park sit vast stretches of forest, most of which at one time or another were the object of logging concessions. Much of Gabon has at one time or another in the last hundred years been logged—mostly for prized hardwood species like padouk. Many of the existing roads in remote parts of the country date back to those logging days. Now, however, with its protected designation, the forest has become the object of scientific research, biological surveys and wildlife management.

Seated in a Toyota Land Cruiser with colleagues from the National Parks Council, a mapping team from the European Union–funded Cybertracker group,[14] and the Ministry of Water and Forests, we jostled around the uneven laterite roads, heading under a canopy-tunnel toward several small villages situated on the eastern border of the park. This was a multipurpose mission, in which I was assessing village educational needs and trying to determine how to help educate the local school children about the importance of conserving the natural world surrounding them. We crossed the Nyanga River, one of the larger rivers of southwestern Gabon; and at one point, we got out to observe the dry-season waterfalls feeding into a tributary of the Nyanga. The falls were impressive, a series of cascading, thunderous monsters, the final fall roughly forty feet tall and just as wide. In the rainy season, the falls wash out, and the river level rises considerably.

Climbing back into the Land Cruiser, we continued on, passing dense forest and occasional grassland savannas. On one of the short, grassy stretches surrounded by forest, we observed several grazing waterbuck, a type of large antelope.

We rolled on until we came to a bridge over another tributary (or maybe the same one) of the Nyanga River, near the village of Doussala. The bridge had been washed out in a flood during the previous rainy season, so we were forced to disembark and wade across the knee-high water with our gear on our backs.

In addition to visiting with schoolteachers to see how we could work with them, one of the other purposes of this mission was to visit a recently erected research camp set up by a team of Japanese anthropologists from the University of Kyoto. (During my time in Gabon, I met several Japanese researchers who were studying primates to glean behavioral and ecological knowledge that, presumably, would assist in our understanding of ourselves.) After walking what I remember as a very long way along an old rutted road, we arrived at a clearing in the forest, which boasted a long, thatched-roof research area, equipped with tables and chairs, charts and localized maps, GPS equipment, sample jars and plastic sacks, and tents.

The researchers had been expecting us, and we shared a quick bite to eat before setting up our own tents. We explained that we would like to follow the researchers on one of their forest transect lines, so that the Cybertracker equipment could be tested on this side of Moukalaba-Doudou National Park. The researchers agreed and said we could join them early the next morning, so we retreated to the tents for some sleep.

The next day, bright and early, the Japanese researchers led us into the forest along a well-worn footpath. These transect lines provided the ability to continuously monitor the same area for observations of wildlife and habitat, which allowed for statistical consistency that could be extrapolated to a larger area. I was not at the time entirely sure of the nature of the research, but I have since learned that the researchers were studying the types and fluctuations of fruits in gorilla habitat,[15] as well as conducting a gorilla habituation project.[16]

For the purposes of my Cybertracker colleagues, they were able to utilize their GPS-enhanced handheld tools to record animal tracks and sightings; vegetation type; human-caused activity, such as timber harvesting and signs of hunting; as well as the geophysical position of each observed sign. Later, the tools would be linked to a computer program, which would plot each observation on a map of the area.

We walked in single file, looking up into the trees, listening for primate calls. Someone signaled quietly for everyone to halt and pointed toward a bare, horizontal branch of an ozigo tree. Squatting low, watching us, was a dark, adult chimpanzee. Although this was not the first time I had seen a chimpanzee, each observation was an awe-inspiring moment. Once this chimpanzee noticed that we had stopped, it scampered along the branch to the trunk of the large tree and disappeared down into the understory. Whether it ran along the ground or fled up into another tree, I never knew.

Pulling my eyes away from the empty space the chimpanzee had recently occupied, I noticed that all of my companions were smiling, as thrilled as I was. The Japanese researchers wrote down notes of time, distance, vegetation type, and estimated size of the primate. My colleagues did much the same with their Cybertracker tools. Then we struck out again along the same transect line, which crisscrossed other transects throughout the walk.

A short time later, I began to smell a strong, musky odor coming from the foliage immediately surrounding us. The researchers and Gabonese whispered, "*Gorille.*" We tiptoed ahead, walking as quietly as possible. The musky smell included the sharp, acrid smell of urine. There was no question that the gorilla knew we were nearby. As explained to me later, the musk and urine smells indicated a fear response to our intrusion. Silently, we continued down the trail. About fifteen feet to my right, a loud crash sounded, accompanied by snapping branches of young saplings and shaking leaves. The sound was moving away from us. We stopped and waited for several minutes, until the leaves stopped moving and the sound abated. This gorilla was gone.

My adrenaline was flowing, and my heart was racing. To be this close to a western lowland gorilla was exhilarating, especially following our earlier experience with our smaller mutual cousin, the chimpanzee. Although I had not actually seen the gorilla, this was almost better; the mystery, the sounds and smells.

After standing stock-still for those long minutes, our little company embarked once again. The researchers said we were nearly finished with the transect, with perhaps half a kilometer left before we would loop back to camp. After a few minutes more of walking, the path turned left, and all around us were saplings of new trees, growing in the space of older growth that had most likely at one time been harvested by loggers. One sapling was roughly ten feet tall, with a strong stem, covered by the thick, long leaves of the Parasolier species. One of the researchers at the front of the line motioned for the rest of us to stop. I caught a whiff of a familiar musky odor. And then, over the top of the leaves, rose a five-fingered, leathery, shiny black hand, thick fingers grasping at a leaf. This amazing, single sighting...a gorilla's hand.

The hand suddenly stopped moving and then quickly dropped from sight in a flurry of leaves and twigs; a strong smell of urine wafted around us as the gorilla shambled off into the deeper forest. All I had seen was that one hand, but the gorilla's presence, not ten feet away from our little troop of observers, lingered on long after the gorilla was gone.

The status of gorilla conservation in Central Africa is one of constant fluctuations, setbacks, successes, and, occasionally, heartaches. Bas Huijbregts, who was the WWF Gamba Project Manager while I was in Gabon, had started a gorilla habituation project north of Setté Cama. He arranged for local and international gorilla experts to survey a small troop over several months to assess whether it would be possible to habituate these lowland gorillas for ecotourism potential (much the same as had been done with mountain gorillas), with the hope of improving local livelihoods while also raising funds for conserving gorillas.

*Peace Corps Volunteers Stanley Dunn and Jason Gray
at entrance of WWF Gorilla Monitoring Forest*

Bas had been in the Congo Basin for many years, working in the Republic of Congo and all over Gabon, before heading up the Gamba office. He was my supervisor and mentor while I worked for WWF, but more importantly, he was—and remains—a close friend. I had spent hours with Bas and others, searching for gorillas near Setté Cama, observing nests and scat. Once, hearkening back to my sighting of the gorilla hand in Moukalaba Doudou National Park, Bas and I were driving back to Gamba from Setté Cama. As we approached Gamba town, I spotted a large, dark form, squatting in the trees about fifty yards from the road. The form looked around, revealing an enormous, muscular back fringed with black and gray fur—my first and only sighting of an adult silverback gorilla! Bas pointed to one of the gorilla's arms, which, from a distance, appeared shorter than the other. He explained that this gorilla was well known in Gamba, because it had lost a hand to a poacher's wire trap.[17] The gorilla associated all humans with this injury, and now, on the rare occasions when it came close to a passing car or truck, it would strike out at the vehicle with its remaining good hand.

After several months of the WWF habituation project near Setté Cama, one of the gorilla experts advised that the project should be halted. Before coming to Gabon, she had spent ten years in the Republic of Congo, working with several gorilla family groups on another habituation project, and a recent Ebola outbreak had decimated the families. Given the risk of human-borne sickness passing to the gorillas, as well as the difficulty of actually seeing them in the dense second-growth forest, combined with this recent tragedy, Bas decided to put the project on indefinite hold. The observations from the team researching the gorillas, and our increasing knowledge of Setté Cama's little troop, reinforced the need to continue striving for better conservation solutions for Gabon's gorillas and their habitat.

Eyes of the Chimpanzee

The old logging road was barely visible beneath the grasses and shrubs that had begun taking it over, as the forest reclaimed its own space. A variety of secondary-growth forest had long since sprouted and now towered above our heads in a full-formed canopy. Sixty-foot-tall okoumé and ozouga trees were visible on either side of the road, as shorter, quicker-growing Parasolier trees sprouted up next to the road. We stood looking down at a shallow, muddy puddle in the middle of the flat cut road, gazing at a series of knuckle-like indentations.

We huddled in a quiet group, absorbing the handprint and the surrounding forest. The group consisted of Richard Carroll, the US World Wildlife Fund Africa Director (and a former Peace Corps volunteer himself), who had many years of experience studying apes in Central Africa; a movie director, exploring the possibility of filming western lowland gorillas and chimpanzees in Gabon; a German doctoral student, studying the distribution of chimpanzees and gorillas in and around Loango and Moukalaba-Doudou National Parks, who was scouting out a new potential study site; and Christian Nzeingui, a Gabonese research assistant who had worked with WWF for several years. And me, the tagalong observer.

Earlier that morning, we had been in Setté Cama village, as Richard and the film director were planning where they would visit to scout potential filming sites. Richard knew the area quite well, as he had been helping fund and manage WWF conservation projects in the region for years. Shortly after dawn, a hoot and laugh broke out from across the Ndougou Lagoon, on the northern shore. Everyone's eyes lit up, and we strained to catch another hint of the awakening chimpanzee troop. The decision was made immediately to cross the one hundred yards of lagoon to the other side, so we could try to track down and observe this noisy troop.

And now, after having boated across and anchored to a mangrove tree, we found ourselves on an old logging road. The puddle showed off a shallow *duiker* print (*duiker* are small forest antelopes), as well as what looked to be a chimpanzee track. We walked down the road, headed west, discussing the various trees and talking softly about possible places to set up camera traps. Then it came again: a loud hoot and holler, off toward the lagoon to our left, echoing back to us through the trees.

Richard Carroll, Christian Nzeingui, and George Butler observing
duiker tracks while looking for chimpanzees

Richard smiled widely and motioned for us to follow him as he left the road and trotted through the understory at a fairly brisk pace. After running diagonally from the road for a few minutes, he called a halt. Then he did an amazing thing. Richard pinched his nose and made a kind of "waouen, waouen" sound, like a loud, crying infant. I recall hearing him explain that *duiker* make this sound after giving birth, and chimpanzees are attracted to the sound in the hopes of feasting on either the protein-rich afterbirth left by the no-longer-pregnant mother antelope or, potentially, on the newborn antelope. Perhaps in response to Richard's vocalization, the hoots and hollers came again, changing direction, and seemed to be headed our way.

Off we went, again following Richard. Jumping over downed tree trunks, around grabbing vines, and sometimes ducking under fallen trees, the hope was to cut the troop off without giving away our presence. After a while, the sounds stopped, and we all came to a silent standstill. Our eyes, ears, and noses were working in overdrive, straining for any sight or sound or smell.

Christian and I heard it first, coming from off to the right. A rustle, then something like feet running. Christian motioned for all of us to duck down behind a tree or anything nearby. I slid against a large tree and flattened myself against its trunk, fringed with thin, loose strips of beige and gray bark. In front of me, the German researcher crouched in a small indentation in the ground, with a horizontal fallen branch in front of him. The others were nearby somewhere. And then I saw something dark run by, followed by a second shape.

I tried to melt into the tree, to become one with its massive, itchy trunk, to hide and yet still be able to see. Time stopped, as did my breathing. One, two, three chimpanzees passed us by; then, strangely, they slowed from an arm and leg run to a walk, as they waited for the rest of the troop to catch up. Neither primate species made so much as a peep, with the chimpanzees quietly meandering along past our hiding place. After those first several went by, I could make out individual hairs on the outstretched arm of a young female, as she stepped lightly from behind a tree, following the leaders. Her face was tan and wrinkled, and her hands, so much like my own, but darker, thicker, more leathery, grasped a nearby shrub for balance, and then she was gone.

About fifteen feet from where we all hid in our nearly single-file line, and directly across from where I was looking, an older chimpanzee paused, looking around, looking straight at me. I only saw its head, with mouth and nose tinged with gray hair, as its lips held a thin, firm line. Round ears stuck out in imitation of mine, large and thin. But the minute its gaze caught mine, I was mesmerized by its dark eyes, brown-black, tinged with amber, and shining in the few sunbeams which made their way through the canopy. Those eyes seemed so wise, and when I tried to drop my gaze so as not to scare it away, I found myself unable to move, so entranced had I become. Those eyes seemed to look through me. Then its gaze lifted, and the chimpanzee straightened, grunted softly, and continued on its way.

Physically and emotionally drained, I wondered if I had imagined that look of wisdom, of recognition. The experience was profound. The troop contained between eight and twelve individuals. As they meandered off in search of food or play, or a place to rest during the hot afternoon hours before building their nests of leaves, branches, and vines, my own troop slowly stood, stretching out backs and sore legs, grinning at how close we had been to such amazing creatures.

The five of us made our way back to the old road, not speaking much, not really needing to. As we trekked to the boat, my mind wandered back to those eyes, to the clarity I had seen within. I think we were all thrilled by the encounter and richer for the observation, but we were also ready to decompress from the adrenaline rush of running through the forest and tracking down these chimpanzees. I knew I was ready for a little rest and food before tackling the next adventure.

Casting Nets

Living near a lagoon means eating a lot of fish. From barracuda (called *bécune* in French) to dorade, Nile perch (called the *Capitaine* in French) to tarpon, the brackish waters bring together fresh and saltwater species, creating an incredible bounty for fishermen and diners.[18] It is hard to beat a fresh-caught tilapia (*carpe* in French) soup in the morning, sitting on the edge of the water where the fish was hooked not ten minutes before. Or a tasty, braised and grilled dorade, covered with hot pepper and spicy tomato and onion sauce, with a side of fried rice or boiled taro. Yet, before one can enjoy such delectable meals, the fish must be transferred from the water into the pot or onto a grill, and the methods of accomplishing that important step are many and varied.

One method is to throw out a baited hook or lure from a boat or shore, either attached to a fishing rod or simply a handheld line. For sports fishermen around the world, this is a familiar tactic; it can sometimes yield a good number of fish for personal, familial, and even communal consumption. A similar method used on the lagoon, which is particularly effective for barracuda, is to sit in a motorized boat (either a pirogue or a boat with a plastic/fiberglass hull) and troll one's hooked and baited line behind the boat as it motors along. Several people can hold fishing rods and hope to catch something, although the greater the number of lines, the more likely that the catch will not be a fish, but another hopeful fisherman's line.

The Ndougou Lagoon boasts a robust sports fishery reputation, including surf casting at the mouth of the lagoon, trolling, and spinner rod and reel, and is well known for its tarpon fishery.[19] Sports fishermen from around the world and from Gamba town frequent the waters. However, to feed the villages, towns, and even the larger cities outside of the Ndougou (including the capital, Libreville), more substantial catching methods are required. The local, traditional fishermen of the Ndougou have perfected several methods that can result in larger catches ready for local markets and the restaurants of Gamba town and beyond.

One of these techniques is similar in function and operation to an ocean-going seiner. A seine is a large net, usually dragged behind a fishing boat that can be brought back upon itself and closed up like a purse (often called a *purse seine*). This method of fishing is used in Alaska for catching summer run salmon. In the Ndougou, the seine method is more person-intensive, partly because it is used in shallow waters and because it does not involve a commercial fishing vessel. Instead, a net, lined with a heavy metal (often lead) filament on the bottom strand, is dropped into the water, while several people, usually men, hold the top filament, effectively blocking passage from the shallow lagoon floor to the surface of the water. The men then walk around, holding the heavy net as tight as possible, and close it up into a purse. This method serves two purposes. First, the movement of the men, as they walk and kick up sand and mud from underneath, acts to chase the fish into the center of the net. Second, as the men close the net, it traps any fish on the inside.

Kassa Ngoma demonstrating fishing techniques

This method is a low-impact, traditional fishing style. The nets cannot be too long, as I can testify from personal experience, because they are very heavy. In addition, they can only be used in water shallow enough to walk in (i.e., no more than about five feet deep). However, the local fishermen know the best areas of the lagoon to step out of their boats and hope for a school of carpe or perch to scoop up in their net. One of the times I was invited along to help catch fish using this method (which requires a certain amount of experience, skill, and strength) was to catch enough fish to feed a funeral ceremony in Setté Cama village. All the fishermen, including me, stripped down to the waist and labored in the murky, muddy waters as we tugged and dragged the heavy net around to make our catch. After several attempts, each of which seemed to take hours, we succeeded only in catching about ten fish in total, mostly carpe, perch, and a dorade. I caught something else as well—a bad sunburn.

Other, less intensive fishing styles include blocking off part of the lagoon, or part of an interior lake or stream, with a net staked in by metal or wooden poles. This net sits against the current, and unsuspecting fish (and sometimes turtles or small crocodiles) get caught and tangled, trapped in place until the fisherman returns to claim his prize. While this stationary net method, similar to gill netting, does result in a greater catch than a simple rod and reel, it seems mostly used for localized consumption, rather than more commercial, artisanal fishing, such as the seine method described previously.

My favorite type of traditional fishing, however, is one method I never actually tried, and I only saw it done a few times in Setté Cama village. It is sometimes called cast netting. The first time I observed this style of fishing, one of the village elders, Jean Mbouity (who liked to be called "l'Américain" and called me "le Gabonais"), stood on the edge of a sunken log jutting out from the shore. In his hands, he held a bunched up tangle of filament nets, wrapped around with a heavy woven cord. He twisted his body to the right, bringing the net around as if to catch himself, and then quickly swung back like he was throwing a large discus. As his body pivoted back to the left, out over the water, he raised his arms and cast out the net, which opened magically, expanding and forming a circle, with the heavy, weighted filament pulling it wide until it hit the water, looking like a gigantic bubble from one of those childhood soapy water bubble toys, or a sparkling, enormous spider web. *L'Américain* held onto the cord, as it rolled out and the net neatly hit the water and sank. He then would pull in the cord, hand over hand, bringing in the full net that had collapsed and captured a few fish inside. Once back on shore, he untangled his catch and then commenced with untangling the cast net and rolling it back into the exact shape and layering needed to repeat the perfect cast.

Every time I ate fish in Gabon, or anywhere, for that matter, I would try to imagine which method of fishing brought me my dinner. It is an amazing thing to reel in your own fish, to feel the fight and understand fully where your meal comes from. It is equally as important to know where fish you did not personally catch come from, to try to figure out who caught it and how, and how your purchase of that meal benefits the fisherman's family—and hopefully, that it is done so as not to negatively impact the waters from whence the fish came. When I cast my own line, whether from a fly rod or a spinner, I am reminded of that expertly cast net, spreading out like an extension of the fisherman, suredly pulling in his next meal.

Trunk in the Water

⌒

T he outboard motor on the metal-hulled boat gave off a hypnotic *whirrr* as it puttered along underwater and propelled us on our way. Raffia swamp lined either side of the narrow river, swaying in the current as weavers flew by. And here we were, traveling upstream, against the current. For the last several days, we had been attending a collaborative working group meeting facilitated by the United States Forest Service's International Program, related to national park management and zoning efforts.[20] A group of us, representing WWF and the local communities from the Ndougou Lagoon on the southern side of Loango National Park, had joined the government, local community, and scientific representatives of the northern side of the park at a wildlife brigade on the Iguela (or N'gove) Lagoon.

To reach Iguela, we had jumped into a boat in Gamba town and ridden an hour and a half up through the Ndougou and then into the offshoot Sounga Lagoon, where we had pulled on heavy packs containing tents, food for a week, clothes, and laptop computers. Then we trekked along an old logging road directly north for several hours before reaching the abandoned village of Inyoungou, where another boat met us to transport us along a narrow river into the Iguela Lagoon (another two-plus hours of transit). We were now headed back home.

The sharp raffia leaves reached out toward the boat, but we sat comfortably, watching the forest ahead start to close in around the swamp. This swamp is abutted by an even larger papyrus swamp, in which great numbers of forest elephants have been observed grazing and forging clear paths through the thick reeds. A tiny tourist camp called Akaka sits at the border of the raffia and papyrus swamps, where the forest juts out on slightly firmer ground.

After a week of technical discussions on management principles and community involvement, all of us felt a sense of accomplishment and a desire to sleep in our beds, rather than on the floor of a tent. And although we did not relish the thought of having to trek back hours in the forest with our packs (now much lighter, as we had eaten up our food supplies), we had a sense of homecoming that I was sure would quicken our steps. The boat pilot assured us we would reach Inyoungou within the hour.

Leaving the raffia swamp behind, we entered a darker, tree-lined section of the river, interspersed with glimpses of dense papyrus. At one point, someone pointed out a solitary elephant, standing well back from the water on the left bank.

The boat motored right on by, and the elephant did not so much as look in our direction.

We rounded a bend in the river, skirting around a submerged root of an ozouga tree, and saw another elephant, this time on the opposite shore. I hastened to grab my camera, hoping to snap a few photos. The elephant was right at the edge of the water, and this one did look at us, startled—and not pleased. It trumpeted out a short burst of air, backing up with its ears flaring, and shook its head from side to side. Then the pilot called out, pointing in front of us about twenty feet. Another elephant was swimming across the narrow river channel! We told the pilot to reverse course, but for some reason, he smiled and headed right toward the swimming mammoth. We shouted some more, and finally he tried to put the motor in reverse, but only succeeded in killing the engine, leaving us floating there in the water, with one angry elephant on the right bank, one swimming not ten feet in front of us, and, still visible behind us, another one on the left bank, watching this all transpire.

One of my WWF colleagues and I grabbed two paddles and backed the boat up to give the swimming creature (and us) more room to maneuver. And there we sat, watching the head of the elephant just above water, hoping the charge feints on the right bank would subside, well aware that we were surrounded. Someone called for us to look behind, as yet another elephant had begun swimming from the right bank to the left, but this one was far enough away that we were not concerned. The elephant in front of us finally reached the far bank and clumsily clambered up the muddy shore, crossing over roots and vines and scrambling up into the papyrus, beyond the trees.

Elephant crossing the river

The perturbed beast to our right headed up the bank until it reached a low spot, presumably where the other swimmer had entered the water. And beyond this elephant, yet another, larger specimen came running out of the forest to see what was causing its kin so much trouble. By this time I was snapping pictures, while simultaneously trying to help the others keep the boat pretty much in place. The pilot was just watching us work, not pitching in at all.

Then, to our complete surprise, the elephant we had originally startled walked out into the river and began swimming in front of us as well. At one point, all that was visible was a periscopic trunk, breathing in air and searching out the far shore. To this day, I am still astonished that the need to cross the river had crept into that animal's brain so strongly that it risked a confrontation with a strange metal object filled with the two-legged rude beings who had caused it such fright. Finally, the elephant finished its swim, climbed up the river bank, and disappeared into the papyrus.

And so we were stuck, unable to work the motor, floating in the calm waters, drifting back down and away from our destination with the slow current. We started taking turns standing in the front of the square-bowed boat, pulling at the water with the oars, inching our way upstream. But after an hour of this arduous work, we had not advanced much more than a few hundred yards, so we decided to disembark on the right bank and hike the rest of the way, leaving our boat pilot to his own devices to make his way back downriver.

Shouldering our packs, we had to struggle through the mud of the papyrus swamp, walking on roots and the occasional hard patch of ground for better footing. Elephant tracks were all around, and at one point during the hike, we spotted four creatures working their way through the reeds. We skirted around them and, after several hours, finally made it to Inyoungou.

The rest of that day turned into a long, difficult, tiring march back through the dark, tripped up by fallen logs and watching out for elephants, until we reached the tiny farming village of Sounga, on the edge of the Sounga Lagoon, well after dark. The village dogs started barking as soon as we got near, and the village chief suspiciously led us through his home toward the boat that had been waiting for us all day. This chief was always suspicious, even though he had helped see us off not a week prior. After making it to our boat, we puttered back toward Gamba, where a hot meal awaited, as did beds and mattresses.

Although I was bruised and battered from the nighttime trek through swamp and forest, I would not have traded anything for that chance to have witnessed forest elephants surround our boat, jump into the water, and extend a snorkel trunk above the water to swim across.

Elephant trunk in the water

Turtle Camp

S itting around the fire, hidden from the wind and low, crashing waves by a sand bluff and beach shrubs and trees, I ate a quick dinner of grilled fish and fried rice, cooked in an old blackened pot and skillet, set on a metal grill over the fire. Above us, a huge blue plastic tarp stretched like a circus tent, with guidelines holding it down to branches and stakes in the ground. A small opening on the far side of the camp led down to a murky backwater lagoon, bordered by mangroves and forest sounds. We sat at a wooden table with wooden benches, like a picnic table, topped with maps, flashlights, dinner plates, metal pinchers, and cattle ear tags; it was like a mad scientist's dinner party. Green two-person tents sat scattered under the tarp, with clothes drying on top, stretched out on the tents and hanging from guidelines. And here I sat, in the midst of this jumble, looking forward to finishing my meal.

On the beaches outside of Gamba town, south of the Shell Gabon main oil terminal, sits Pont Dick, a beach frequented by families and beachgoers on the weekend. It is about a fifteen- to twenty-minute taxi ride from Gamba. This beach is also the site of an ongoing marine turtle research project; and here, for six months out of every year, situated in a secluded area far from the main foot traffic, lies the turtle camp.

Comprised of researchers from various universities, WWF, the European Union–funded Protomac, and the local nonprofit Ibonga, the turtle camp is a specialized research camp, conducting ecological, genetic, and physiological studies on the five species of marine turtles that nest on the coasts of Gabon: the leatherback, the green turtle, the loggerhead turtle, the olive ridley turtle, and the hawksbill turtle. The Pont Dick turtle camp also plays host to tourists, school groups, and visiting friends. However, no matter who is visiting (or not), these dedicated turtle researchers[21] stick to a schedule dictated by the tides, walking the 5.75-kilometer study zone several times a day (and night) to observe, monitor, tag (with the numbered cattle ear tags mentioned earlier), and protect the ancient reptiles of the sea and their precious eggs from poachers.

After supper on this particular evening, one of the researchers looked over the high-tide schedule. He explained that the turtles would come at high tide, helped along by the strength of the waves to get up into the sand, where they could then start their climb higher up onto the beach to dig a nest and deposit their eggs out of reach of the chilly waters. Supper was often timed to coincide with the tide as well, so the team could fuel up before heading out. I decided to join the two Ibonga researchers, who were covering the southern end of the study zone. The other half of the team would walk to the northern edge.

As we set out, we checked to make sure our headlights and handheld flashlights were in working order. The lights would only be used to inspect nests and observe actual nesting behavior, but would otherwise be left dark, so as not to confuse turtles as they left or returned to the sea. The night was humid, as always, with a soft breeze and the rumbling, splashing sounds of waves lapping at our feet. I enjoyed walking just at the tide line, with the occasional wave cooling off my bare feet. The researchers usually walked higher up, to increase their chances of running into fresh turtle tracks.

As we walked, the salty breeze brought decaying leaf and musky elephant smells to our nostrils, reminding us to keep a sharp eye out for any grazing pachyderms. Walking into the wind kept our scents away from any passing animals but made it hard to determine where the smells we caught were coming from. We saw no elephants that night.

Wet sand found its way in between my toes and, with the help of the wind, gritted itself into every crease of my body. It had taken me a while to become used to the mix of humidity-induced sweat, sand, salt, and comfort. By the time I joined the team that night, though, I barely noticed the sand anymore.

The beach was mostly flat, but an occasional sand drift would grow out of the terrain in front of us, caused by an extra-large wave, or perhaps a buried log, shielding the way ahead behind a small sand dune. And sometimes, especially after a heavy rain, the narrow lagoon behind the beach would overflow, emptying into the ocean and opening up a shallow streambed. No matter the obstacle, the research-walk continued, over logs and hills, through streams, and onward. The fact that the study area was so small might have given the twice-daily hikes an overly monotonous feeling. However, on the many nights I participated in this work, and according to the researchers who did this for six months straight, each hike brought new sights and new opportunities to glimpse nature at its most primal, beautiful self.

As we crossed a stream, one of my friends pointed up toward the beach, where he said the team had observed a leatherback laying eggs a few days before. We ran across some worn tracks leading up to a messy, swept-looking spot of sand high on the beach. Often, the turtles will dig a nest a few feet deep, then cover it up without laying any eggs, only to drag themselves a few feet away to dig another nest and lay their small, drab-white eggs inside. This was a defense mechanism designed to fool predators such as egg-stealing red-capped mangabey monkeys (an old world primate endemic to this area of Gabon), monitor lizards, marsh mongoose, civets, and genets, and to give their eggs a better chance at hatching. This tactic could also sometimes fool the research team, but only for a little while. On that particular night, the team had dug down in each nest, to determine which was real, and then posted three wooden stakes into the ground, so it would be visible in the morning, when measurements could be made and the true number of viable nests counted more accurately.

Onward we went. Each half of the turtle team also carried walkie-talkies; the latest model was one I had brought back from a trip home to Montana the previous Christmas. These served a potentially vital function of alerting the whole team of an injury to a researcher, or to ask for help with a particularly large turtle specimen. My group turned ours on from time to time to see if any news came across from the northward-bound researchers.

I had fallen back with one of the researchers, chatting about the long hours these stalwart conservationists put into the turtle work, when the other researcher called to us from ahead to hurry and catch up. A fresh set of tracks, much narrower than the leatherback prints, led from the ocean up to the sand and, perhaps ten feet further south, back into the sea. An olive ridley turtle had nested perhaps an hour before and had already returned to swim in the ocean. We squatted down next to the nest (there was no false nest this time) and marked it with wooden sticks found higher on the beach. The turtle gurus measured the nest quickly, and I marveled at the way the turtle had dragged itself with its flippers upward from the water. Then we continued on. No time for a leisurely stroll on this research project!

Olive ridley turtles pull themselves along, one flipper at a time, creating an off-kilter track, unlike the even, tractor-like prints of a leatherback, which pulls itself using both front flippers at the same time. The visual effect of this difference, when the turtle is actually moving, is a fast, jerky, robotlike quickness for the smaller olive ridley, compared to a slower, stronger, more laborious struggle for the leatherback. This is likely also a consequence of the weight difference, as olive ridleys weigh in at about one hundred pounds, whereas a leatherback may weigh anywhere from one thousand to two thousand pounds.[22]

We walked on for another forty minutes, reaching the end of the study area, which was marked by a large, partially buried log. Sitting near the log, resting a little while, we all drank water from our plastic water bottles, replenishing some of the moisture that we had sweat out in the humid night air. Someone mentioned that he hoped we would see a nesting turtle on the way back to the camp, and I wholeheartedly agreed.

So back we went, retracing our footsteps, headed north to our tents and to sleep. On the way, we watched for new tracks and signs of turtle activity. Our luck was with us that night, because not thirty minutes later, we found a set of leatherback tracks headed up the beach. Following these deep prints, we soon came upon a female turtle, which was nearly finished with digging her nest. She would brace her huge body, pulling herself forward with both flippers, then pushing back into the sand, as if swimming through the white grains, powerfully pushing her way deeper and throwing mounds of sand behind her and onto us.

Occasionally, she would maneuver her rear flippers to dig and push sand out of a smaller hole within the larger nest, or to reposition herself, sometimes stopping for a few seconds to breathe deeply before digging again. She would exhale in grunts and low hisses. And in a celebrated, protective adaptation, she shed thick, gooey tears throughout the nesting process. These turtle tears keep sand out of an egg-laying turtle's eyes and also help her to release excess salt. However, to a casual observer, they are easy to interpret as both tears of labor pains and tears of joy from helping the species survive.

Finally, after watching her push and fight the sand for several long minutes, one of the researchers turned on his flashlight and stepped behind her, motioning for me to come and look. She had stopped moving the front part of her body, and now she gently squeezed small, round white egg after egg into the small hole dug by her rear flippers. Out they fell, landing softly on the sand, and then on each other, to be buried for a nearly two-month incubation.[23] In all, she laid nearly seventy eggs, of which probably more than half were "false," or yolkless, eggs—another strategy to confuse predators and ensure that at least some viable eggs hatch.[24]

For some nestings, the turtle researchers would actually transfer the eggs from the nest as the turtle laid them, reaching down into the nest to remove the eggs and place them into a sand-lined bucket so the team could "renest" them in a protected enclosure near the turtle camp, to study hatch success rates and temperature differences on the sex of the young hatchlings, and to further guarantee that at least some young turtles made it back to sea. But on this night, the three of us just measured this brave mother's shell, tagged her with a numbered metal tag on her rear right flipper (some turtles were also tagged with a tiny, insertable, scannable tag called a PIT tag), and stepped back to watch as she diligently covered up the nest, patted down the entire area to again confuse predators, and lumbered back to the waters of the Atlantic.[25] One of the turtles tagged on Pont Dick in 2003 was actually caught by a fisherman off the coast of Argentina in 2005, emphasizing the importance of tagging turtles, even with simple metal bands, to better understand their migration. Similar, more sophisticated taggings include satellite transmitters fitted to turtle backpacks.

I smiled at my friends, these stalwart researchers, and we resumed our walk toward camp, after having marked the nest with branches. When we reached camp, the other half of the team was already asleep. And because the turtle team walked this same route each morning, looking for any nests they missed the night before, we would be up in a few hours to walk the same section of sandy beach again. I opened up my tent, climbed in, and closed up the zipper to keep out mosquitoes, before falling into a deep, exhausted, happy sleep. Such was a night in the life of a marine turtle conservationist.

One of my favorite things to do at the turtle camp, with the researchers, was to organize field trips with some of the schoolchildren from Gamba town, many of whom had never seen sea turtles in the wild. A lot of Gabonese children, especially along the coast, have eaten poached turtle eggs and sometimes even turtle meat, but most had never been taken to the beach at night to see a nesting turtle, let alone to participate in research activity. This educational, life-changing experience was an excellent opportunity to assist in the reduction of endangered marine turtle poaching, while creating an exciting adventure for the students and a great opportunity for the local researchers to show off their knowledge, skill, and dedication.

So, once parental consent was granted, I would organize WWF vehicles, taxis, anything on hand, to bring a wide-eyed, excited bunch of teenagers out to the beach so near to their homes. Seeing the sheer wonder in their eyes when we came across a leatherback as she laid her eggs in the wet sand, and seeing the pride on a local researcher's face as he explained his work—these are some of my favorite memories of Gabon.

Student posing with leatherback turtle near Gamba

Part V: Educating the Students and the Teacher

> In the end, we will conserve only what we love. We will love only what we understand. We will understand only what we are taught.

> —BABA DIOUM

Enfants du Quartier

While walking back to my host family's home in the Isaac neighborhood of Lambaréné, I often took shortcuts through people's yards and the small footpaths over little streams that all of the locals used. This offered me a wonderful opportunity to experience daily life in different areas of town and to sort of peek in on different families' lives. I would come across people doing their laundry in plastic buckets with soap and water, or cooking *beignets* and fish in huge amounts of palm oil; or I might surprise a bunch of children, playing soccer in the sand between their homes.

Once in a while, I came across children who had never before seen a white person. There was one little boy in particular, probably two years old, who would look at me as if I were the most hideous monster he had ever seen. He would see me from afar, start crying and screaming, and run away. For the better part of two weeks, this became a kind of ritual, where the boy's family—his older siblings, mostly—would wait for me on the small footpath and motion for me to slow down. Then they would run back to make sure their little brother was out in the yard. As I approached, he would start to shake and then scream out that a monster was coming, and the whole family would burst into laughter. I think he eventually got used to me walking by, because he stopped screaming, and eventually—once—even smiled.

Children were constantly playing, running, curious. They would sit with their parents and listen to stories around the cook fire. They would join in on singing and dancing as if it were the most important thing in the world (perhaps it was). And they were quick to become friends with the strange *ibamba* (white person) who was now living in their midst. Once I settled into life in Gamba, I became a hit attraction with the *enfants du quartier* (neighborhood kids). My home had a small cement front patio, covered by a metal awning that was supported by two metal posts. I often sat out on this porch playing my guitar, or enjoying the sounds of the family that owned most of the homes in the neighborhood as they practiced for a traditional ceremony, cooked their supper, and went about their daily activities. When I played my guitar, the children would start to come over, laughing and joking about the color of my hair, my height, and my big Peace Corps–issued glasses.

I once made the mistake of inviting them all in to play, which resulted in a messy, chaotic invasion of my space, and their parents subsequently suggested I limit the kids to the porch outside. *Excellent idea*, I thought. So we would play outside; I would show them photos of Montana and of parts of Gabon I had visited, and they would talk about their schoolwork or their trip to the village over the weekend. And they would dance to my guitar or to the little stereo I bought on a trip to Libreville. Curious pranksters with names like Gateaux, Gaga, Madame, Orphée, and Kenny were always visiting my house.

Neighborhood kids standing outside my porch acting for the camera

I loved their smiling faces, with their missing teeth and bright eyes, and found it amusing that the youngest were unceasingly fascinated that I had hairs on my arms and legs. (Many people in Gabon have nearly hairless arms and legs, so the fact that the tall white guy was somewhat hairy was a great source of amazement and amusement for these kids).

Interestingly, one of my neighbors had a pet red-capped mangabey monkey named Daouda that was also fascinated with the hairs on my arms. Daouda would sit on my shoulder or hold onto me around the neck and pull at the hair on my forearm for half an hour at a time.

My neighbor and counterpart, Jean Pierre, had two sons, Dan and Dylan, who loved coming over to my house; and they became my little shadows, trying to wear my shoes and falling asleep on my rattan couch. When the youngest (Dylan) would need a diaper change, I carried him back over to his mother, Angelique, who laughed and said I would have to learn to change diapers someday. If the boys were causing a ruckus or playing too rough, all of our neighbors would step in to separate them and verbally discipline them, or occasionally give them a light swat on the backside. The cliché phrase applied to raising children throughout the world holds quite true in Gabon—it does take a village to raise a child.

And all of these kids, well-behaved or not, were such a fixture in my life in Gabon, in Gamba town, and in Setté Cama village that my recollections of so many events are infused with images of little kids running this way and that, trying to help out or simply being present.

Children were often the topic of conversation, too, as nearly everyone either had a child or was someone's aunt or uncle, older brother or sister. And some children were discussed more than others. Once, when discussing a family who had recently had twins, Jean Pierre started talking about the cultural aspects of children, names, and how they relate to animals. He started by explaining to me that the hippopotamus and the elephant are spiritual and metaphorical twins. These largest of mammals in Gabon represent beings from the same mother, evidenced by their near-identical skin color, size, power, and ivory tusks. He told me that in certain Gabonese ethnic groups, and clans within the ethnic group, it is forbidden to hunt and consume certain animals, which are taken as totems of the clan. And some animals, such as the hippo and the elephant, are viewed as the same creature; meaning that if a clan has taken the elephant as its totem, then clan members cannot hunt or eat hippos either. This same connection is thought to exist between the black mamba and the green mamba.

I have to admit that the differences between a clan and an ethnic group are beyond my understanding. Try as I might to delve into this topic, I have made little headway into comprehending where the lines are and when one person of the Bapunu ethnic group may be in the same clan as a person from the Gishira ethnic group. However, Jean Pierre was emphatic that this notion of twins within the spiritual, animal world carried across ethnic and clan lines. And in many African cultures, human twins also carry a special significance.[26]

Famously, Chinua Achebe's *Things Fall Apart* touched on the stigma of twins and the ritual abandonment of such newborns in the part of Nigeria discussed in that book. In Gabon, Jean Pierre said that twins are infused with a power to be respected, desired, and feared. I found this fascination with twins, well...fascinating. It was a common belief that before a woman gave birth to twins, someone in the family would have a dream, indicating that twins were coming and announcing their names.[27] For instance, some human twins carry the names of twin animals such as *Nzaou* (elephant in Yilumbu) and *Mfoubou* (hippo in Yilumbu).[28] Coincidentally, Jean Pierre and Angelique had twins (a boy, Dereck, and a girl, Doriana) a few years after I left.

In any case, whether twins or not, children play a central role in life in Gabon, much as they do in life everywhere. One difference between life in Gabon and the United States that many Peace Corps volunteers experienced is the fact that children have a great deal of respect for and willingness to assist their elders. One can send a child to the market to bring back food or drink, and the child's parents expect their offspring to do this work without question. When friends would visit, and I ran out of rice or even beer, I could call on any of the neighborhood kids to come over and ask them to help me out. They would smile and say "of course," and I would give them enough money to buy whatever I was needing, along with a little extra for some treat, and the child would run off and bring me back what I asked for. This was called "sending the little one," or *"envoyer le petit."* Now, try to imagine sending your neighbor's child, without asking your neighbor, to the market to pick you up some fruit or a six-pack of beer. Or scolding your neighbor's child for some misbehavior. This would, of course, be frowned upon in the United States (especially the beer part). But in Gabon, it was the norm.

Jean Pierre encouraged his boys to spend time with their *Tonton* (Uncle) Jason, and Dan and Dylan really did feel like little nephews. They made me laugh, as they played together on my porch, or when they asked (in obviously false shyness) whether they could come in to play. I say false shyness, because those boys were very bold! And they taught me patience, as they would squabble as only brothers can do—Dan complained about Dylan taking his toys, and Dylan, too young to speak, would start crying. When I couldn't cheer them up, only their dad would do—scooping them up, getting them to laugh, all better.

When I think about all those *enfants du quartier*, and my little shadow Bayet boys, all of whom definitely played a critical role in my life in Gabon, I cannot help but think that although it may take a village to raise a child, those children certainly helped raise me.

Classroom Challenges

⤫

Dark rain clouds rolled in low on the horizon, pulling the heat of the day up and off the dirt street, breathing it in, seeming to swish it around and swallow it whole. Jean Pierre and I were dressed in our work clothes (beige slacks and short-sleeved, collared shirts) and were pedaling quickly on our bikes toward l'Ecole Bilingue, one of the primary schools in Gamba. I looked out at the clouds and yelled out that we needed to hurry, or we would surely get soaked. Jean Pierre grinned, said nothing, and kept on peddling at the same brisk pace. We arrived at the edge of Bilingue, which was situated at the bottom of a small hill, with a sand courtyard, squat, low buildings with slats of wood for windows, and dark rooms. Children ran and played in the courtyard, watched over by their teachers.

We climbed off our bikes and walked them through the sandy yard onto the cement walkway that lined the classrooms.

The teachers whistled to the students to form orderly lines and prepare to reenter their respective classrooms. Bilingue (which purported to teach both English and French) was a private school (meaning the parents paid slightly more for the classes, uniforms, and materials than for a public school), with primary and secondary classes. Jean Pierre and I had started an environmental education program through Ibonga, the local nonprofit he had founded several years previously, with all of the primary schools in Gamba for the fourth- and fifth-grade-level school children (CM1 and CM2 in the Gabonese/French system, meaning Classe Moyene 1 and Classe Moyene 2), and we made a circuit to hit every CM1 and CM2 class in every school at least once every other week.

On this day, we carried the usual Ibonga brochures, discussing the importance of habitat and of disposing of garbage properly, as well as some large sheets of poster paper with basic environmental concepts sketched out for our lessons. These lessons included discussions about water, national parks, insects, and mammals. Though not on this day, we would also often invite researchers from the Smithsonian Institution, government officials from the Ministry of Waters and Forests, and even local fishermen to discuss their work with the students.

Jean Pierre and I became sort of celebrities with the students, partly because we sometimes organized field trips, but most likely because we were not their full-time teachers and did not make them take tests. Eventually, the lessons we taught (with permission from the school principals and teachers) would help to create an official curriculum of environmental education integrated into math, biology, and other courses. But that came later.

We parked our bikes outside the classroom of the day's lesson, as the children all went inside and sat down at their desks. The clouds still rolled in, without any raindrops yet falling. I taped our lesson sheet up on the blackboard, made from smooth-cut pieces of the okoumé tree, while Jean Pierre led the class in singing a song he had developed for Ibonga, which the children loved. While the students sang, I could pass out handouts or start writing on the board.

Ibonga Theme Song[29]

We are the united and courageous youth
Of Ibonga, always engaged
In the understanding and the protection
Of the environment

Our duty is to fight against pollution
And to ensure the sustainable use of our
natural resources
Always concerned about seeing any
endangered species
And making sure we have a healthy
environment

So ladies and gentlemen, please help Ibonga
for the future
Of the Complex of Protected Areas in the
Southwest of Gabon

*As we march on, happily, this is why we
walk proudly
For we have decided to fight against all
environmental problems.*

*Because Nature, with all of her flora and
fauna, is very precious*

We had developed this tag-team-style teaching for several reasons. Many of the classes we taught in held over ninety students. That is a lot of children to try to focus on the lesson of the day. (Some of my Peace Corps colleagues told me they had over one hundred students in some of their classes!) In addition, the classrooms did not usually have any electricity, meaning that on hot days, it got very hot, and on cloudy days, the lighting was not always the best. Finally, when I first arrived, many of the students had never had a funny-sounding, non-African teacher before. Our partnership worked very well—I helped Jean Pierre develop lessons and become more organized, and he helped me integrate into the school system and into the community.

The genius of the Ibonga song was that it helped the class focus, providing them with an entertaining activity while also calming them down after their recess outside. Another great trick I learned from Jean Pierre was to have the students stand up, then sit down, calling out "stand, sit, stand, sit, sit," and watching the class laugh as some remained seated per the command, while others stood. It was another simple way for students to release steam and focus.

As we started the lesson, with me taking over to give the introduction and Jean Pierre preparing some examples on our lesson papers of conservation jobs in the area, the rain hit. And by *hit*, I mean hard. It came down in sheets, hitting the corrugated metal roof of the classroom, drowning out all other sound, including our lesson. The rain clouds hung so low that it became nearly as dark as night. Rain blew in through the wooden slats, so the children seated nearest to these open "windows" had to move closer to the center of the room to keep themselves and their school supplies from getting wet.

I learned a simple fact of life that the teachers and students in Gabon had long since known: you just have to wait it out. During the rainy season in Gabon, rains often come down hard, but they often quickly relent and move away as the sun burns away the clouds. If they do not relent, then everyone eventually makes a mad dash home, inevitably becoming soaked, as the roadways flood and the mud builds up.

Luckily, the rain and clouds dissipated after ten minutes or so, and our lesson resumed (after a few "stand, sit, stand, stand" exercises). It still amazes me how resilient those students and teachers are, faced with very difficult circumstances, from very little to no infrastructure to extreme weather conditions. And yet they continued on with their pursuit of knowledge and understanding, with their willingness to listen to Jean Pierre and me expound upon the importance of protecting the environment that sometimes puts those same difficult circumstances directly in their paths.

The classes we taught, I hope and believe, were valuable for those ninety-plus students in that classroom, and the hundreds more in other classes. Beyond a shadow of a doubt, I know that the lessons those children taught me—those of patience, perseverance, and acceptance—continue to impact my life every day.

Jason Gray teaching environmental education class
at Lorésie School in Gamba

Excursions and Expeditions

"Wow!" exclaimed one of the students. He looked up at me and grinned broadly. I had just shown him how to adjust the focus on a microscope, something he had never had the opportunity to look through before; he had just experienced his first up-close look at the multiple eyes of a large fly. Looking around, I smiled broadly as well. This was a good day.

Several months before, Jean Pierre and I had convinced Michelle Lee, of the Smithsonian Institution, that the schoolchildren of Gamba and its surrounding villages would really benefit from the participation of her team of local experts as part of our Ibonga classes. This wasn't a hard thing to convince her of, and she and her researchers were extremely generous of their time, expertise, and familiarity with the local ecology. They assisted us in developing lesson plans and in coteaching classes to the primary schoolchildren. In fact, several of the

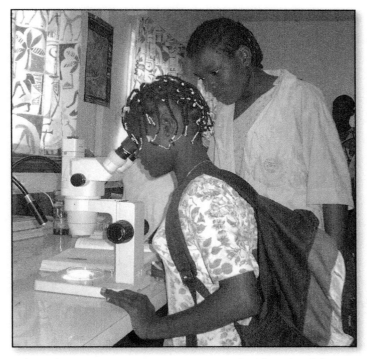

Students learning to use a microscope at Smithsonian laboratory

Smithsonian researchers had children in the same classes we were teaching.

After a few months of this collaboration, Michelle offered up another teaching opportunity, better than simple classroom lessons. The Smithsonian had set up a laboratory in a building several kilometers from town. As with many Smithsonian facilities, this lab served as a sort of museum/storehouse for many biological specimens, as well as a site where visiting researchers could conduct their nonfield work. The lab had amassed the largest collection of Central African insects in Gabon, a treasure trove for Ibonga's students!

Jean Pierre and I spoke with the school directors and teachers and designed a field trip program to the lab. Students were required to obtain parental consent, and we would alternate between schools, so that each class we taught was able to visit the lab for a several-hour visit at least once a year. With Smithsonian and WWF vehicles, and occasional taxis (Gamba did not have any school buses), Jean Pierre and I would haul the students and their teachers over to the lab. We helped set up chairs, so the students could sit through a kind of show-and-tell lecture, in which our Smithsonian colleagues took turns discussing the different animals they had studied in the field and in the lab. Our students could see these specimens, including the ever-popular poisonous snakes.

One of the lab managers loved to ask, "Who here has seen a black mamba before?" Nearly every hand went up from his rapt audience. "Are you sure?" he'd ask.

"*Oui, monsieur!*" came the enthusiastic response. Yes, sir, we have.

Pausing mischievously, he would quickly reach into a freezer in the lecture hall and pop out a frozen black mamba. He then thrust it toward the students, laughing as he asked, "Have you seen one from this close?"

The students would burst out laughing, as some shrank away and others leaned forward. Most were brave enough to touch it.

This room also included boxes full of measured, marked, and stuffed reptiles, bats, and bird specimens, including rosy bee-eaters, weavers, kingfishers, and many others. The Smithsonian had even collected skulls of hippos, elephants, and primates.

In an adjoining building, the researchers had organized dozens of waist-high shelves, filled with pull-out boxes full of beetles, flies, millipedes, spiders, scorpions, and thousands of other fascinating creatures from around the region. The boxes were covered in glass, so the students could decide which insects or arachnids they most wanted to see. The researchers would prepare a few specimens and bring them over to a row of microscopes, where the students could line up, learn how to use these essential scientific tools, and exclaim in wonder as this tiny world jumped into magnification.

Each trip to the lab brought new excitement, both from the students and their teachers. It gave the local Smithsonian experts a chance to teach their friends' children (or even their own) and to hone their own teaching skills. And it provided Jean Pierre and me with an excellent way to encourage our classes to better appreciate the complexity and diversity of their region. With the full-time teachers, we would prepare lesson plans for the next classes, where we'd follow up with questions to the children about their favorite part of the visit, what they thought about the microscopes, and about science generally.

The lab visits were only part of our field trip program. Seeing how much the students enjoyed these off-school-ground trips, we worked through Ibonga on other types of excursions, including student-led town cleanup campaigns, where the students picked up trash from the streets and neighborhoods to ensure that their town was free from debris, visits to the marine turtle research camp, and even beach cleanups. These activities engaged not only the students but also their parents, providing hands-on experience to complement the classes they received at school.

Ibonga's most popular field trip was designed for secondary school students from Gamba's high school. This was famously called the *"Expédition"* (the Expedition). Every summer, around late July to early August, Ibonga organizes a week to two-week camping trip for a group of twelve to twenty high school students to Setté Cama. The students apply for these limited places. They must demonstrate their commitment to Ibonga and to environmental issues by participating through-out the year in the town cleanups and in their own activities such as art and culture contests. They must convince their parents of the importance of keeping their neighborhoods clean and of the other lessons learned throughout the year, and they must obtain permission to attend the Expedition. Finally, the applicants must promise to fully engage in the chores of maintaining a camp; cooking and cleaning; study-ing their lessons; and respecting the speakers, villagers, and each other. Jean Pierre and I also insisted on having an equal number of boys and girls, to emphasize the importance of equal education and responsibility.

Once we had a full group of *expéditionaires*, Jean Pierre and I would start fundraising. We obtained much support from the local wildlife brigade, WWF, the Smithsonian, and from

Shell Gabon, which furnished boat fuel and an organized visit during the Expedition to an oil well. The Smithsonian and the wildlife officials demonstrated their research techniques, including mist nets for catching birds and bats, to determine which species were present, and bucket trap lines on the ground, to assess rodent and reptile species.

We also received invaluable assistance from the village of Setté Cama, which allowed the camp to exist for several weeks right outside the village and interacted with the Ibonga students throughout the summer by organizing fishing trips, soccer matches, and cultural events with the village elders, including visits to palm wine plantations and discussions of traditional medicine.

The most anticipated activity of these Expeditions was a visit to Loango National Park. Many of the students had participated in Ibonga's classes during primary school. They had heard our lessons about Gabon's national parks, and this was the first time many would visit one.

By the end of the summer, the students had formed strong bonds with each other, with the villagers, and with Ibonga. The Expedition is still one of Ibonga's annual activities, and all of Ibonga's field trip excursions have helped cement an awareness of environmental issues in the students, parents, and population of Gamba, Setté Cama, and the surrounding region.

Hand-Pulled Ferry of Boumé Boumé

❧

"Ah, ça," muttered Guy Noël Djoumtsi, one of the WWF drivers.

Steam poured up and out from under the Toyota Land Cruiser's hood. The angry sun beat down on our heads like a furious drummer, tapping away with increasing energy and heat. I stood off to the side of the vehicle, dipping my baseball cap into the muddy waters underneath the vehicle, soaking it and placing it on my overheated head, grateful for the brief sense of coolness. We were almost there, almost out of the Ouanga Plains to the Boumé Boumé crossing. Almost, but not yet. That last stretch of wet sand leading into the deep pool of murky water seemed so far away, and Guy Noël had gunned the engine to get us passed this last puddle. The puddle became a moat, blocking our passage as the mud reached up and grabbed the tires. Guy Noël kept at it for a few minutes, trying to accelerate, turning the wheels this way and that, to no avail. We were good and stuck, and the steam from under the hood more than hinted at an overheated engine.

So we all piled out—Jean Pierre, several Gamba primary school principals, Ibonga staff, and I. These principals were also expert trainers of teachers. We were headed to Tchibanga to conduct a teacher training with nearly sixty teachers and education officials from all over the neighboring Nyanga Province. First, though, we had to survive the road to Tchibanga. Luckily, like my friend Demsey, who could fix broken struts with branches, Guy Noël knew how to drive this road.

He said we would wait a few minutes before trying to push again to dislodge the vehicle. In the meantime, he poured water into the radiator to cool it down. When planning a trip like this one, it is important to factor extra hours in to account for mishaps, getting stuck, and other road hazards. So none of us was much perturbed by this puddle. Plus, it was a nice break from the bumpy ride we had just overcome, and the one we knew was coming further along the road. Sure enough, after a few minutes, the engine cooled, and Guy Noël started up the motor. The rest of us strolled into the shallow water and pushed from behind, conscious of the fact that we would all likely get a little muddy. We pushed and, miraculously, the mud gave way, and the truck made it through.

After climbing back into the Land Cruiser, we puttered along to the river crossing at Boumé Boumé. This crossing is maybe sixty or seventy feet wide. On the east side of the road sits an unfinished bridge. So the only way to get a vehicle to the other side sat floating on the water, on the far bank: the ferry of Boumé Boumé. This is no ordinary ferry with a motor and crew. No, this ferry is a flat metal contraption with two ramps on either side to allow for a single vehicle to carefully make its way onto and off of the ferry. And the marvelous contraption is strung across the river by a thick woven rope on one side and a thin metal cable on the other. With the rope, travelers must actually pull themselves across the river.

We jumped out of the truck and started hauling in the rope to bring the ferry across to our side. The river current was not too strong, but pulling a heavy metal barge across was a good workout. After a few minutes, the ferry was on our side. We paused to cool off some more, and Guy Noël dipped his hand in the muddy waters for a quick drink. Although this is not the most sanitary thing to do, many Gabonese had impressed upon me the importance of drinking in at least a little water before crossing a stream, creek, or river. This seems to signify a certain respect for the water and an implicit request for passage. In any case, I followed suit, though I most often just dampened my forehead and face, without drinking in the water.

While we held the ferry steady, Guy Noël positioned the Land Cruiser and expertly maneuvered it up on to the narrow metal bed of the ferry. We all climbed on, and I helped pull us across while Guy Noël filled up his plastic water jug with river water to further cool down the radiator. Hand over hand, we pulled, laughing nervously as the front end of the ferry started flooding slightly. The car sat roughly in the center, for better balance, and so we (hopefully) would not sink.

"*Tirez,*" I yelled, joking with Jean Pierre that the old women in the village could pull harder than him. He smiled and kept on pulling, teasing me that he was actually doing all of the work—which, I'll admit, was probably true.

Jason Gray and Guy Noël Djoumtsi crossing the Nyanga River at the hand-pulled ferry of Boumé Boumé

After about ten minutes of careful, steady pulling, we lowered the front ramps onto the sandy shore of the south side and stepped off the ferry to hold it steady while Guy Noël once more expertly wheeled our transportation off of the ferry and back to semidry land. We pulled the ferry up a little higher onto the shore, so it would not sit floating and risk becoming tangled—or worse yet, being carried away by the current. Without this simple, human-powered ferry, vehicle traffic to and from Gamba would cease; and as we were due to return home in less than a week, we wanted to make sure that we at least did our part to ensure the road stayed open.

Someone jokingly said, "*Ah, notre pays, le Gabon*" (Ah, our country, Gabon).

We all looked from the unfinished bridge to the ferry and back, nodding our heads in agreement, amazement, and acceptance. This was the way it was; and we, like so many others, had once again made it across the river to continue our way along the national highway toward the group of teachers waiting to be trained in Gabon's emerging environmental education curriculum.

We checked to make sure all of our gear was securely fastened to the top of the Land Cruiser, checked the tires, and jumped back in after looking one more time at this river crossing, the hand-pulled ferry of Boumé Boumé.

I assisted Ibonga conduct several teacher trainings while I was in Gabon. These trainings were designed to help local elementary school teachers and directors become comfortable with environmental education subjects and techniques, so they could present lessons to their students, and also train their fellow teachers. The first training took place in Gamba for the schools around the Ndougou Lagoon; it taught various techniques of incorporating environmental themes into existing lessons. Ibonga was assisted by local Ministry of Education officials, as well as speakers from the Ministry of

Water and Forests, National Parks Council, WWF, Smithsonian Institution, and local farmers. Each participant (from seven schools in Gamba and the schools from all of the villages around the lagoon) was provided with teaching materials, such as maps, new textbooks that included activities related to conservation and farming, and more direct contact with each other to help design and prepare their own lesson planning, in preparation for an emerging national environmental curriculum and exams.

This initial training proved quite successful, and Ibonga was invited to host a larger training in Tchibanga. For the second training, WWF and the Peace Corps helped provide logistical and technical support (in the form of a volunteer trainer), and Ibonga received grant support from WWF, USAID, and the Dutch Central African Poverty Alleviation Programme. Once we had survived the journey over the hand-pulled ferry of Boumé Boumé, we picked up teachers along the way, transporting them to Tchibanga for a three-day session with the local representatives of the Ministry of Education, environmental and national parks officials, and Ibonga trainers.

This second training was provided to fifty-seven trainees from dozens of villages around the Nyanga Province and from Tchibanga town. As in the Setté Cama training, each participant was provided with extra teaching materials, including copies of textbooks, maps, lesson-planning samples, and a suite of new contacts from their regional environment and national park agencies.

Ibonga continues to work with these schools and their teachers, directors, and students. The organization also continues to provide education services to schools around Gamba, as well as supporting the ongoing development of the national environmental education curriculum.[30]

Part VI: Tourism, Culture, and Love

Travel is fatal to prejudice, bigotry, and narrow-mindedness, and many of our people need it sorely on these accounts. Broad, wholesome, charitable views of men and things cannot be acquired by vegetating in one little corner of the earth all one's lifetime.

—MARK TWAIN, *THE INNOCENTS ABROAD*

A nation's culture resides in the hearts and in the soul of its people.

—MOHANDAS KARAMCHAND GANDHI

Hippos in the Ndougou

T he water shone like a mirror, glassy and clear, reflecting the clouds above and the drooping mangroves hanging from the shore line. The lagoon meandered up into the mangroves, snaking like a silver line, a tide-controlled river of brackish water, now reflecting the sunlight, and the next minute dark with mud and matter from decaying leaves. These waters were rich in fish—carp, barracuda, dorade. From the far shore, closer to the ocean, a green and violet hadada ibis called its creaking squawk, as if to rouse its neighboring birds from their nighttime slumber. After many mornings awakening to this same call, the song of this particular ibis species grated on my nerves like fingernails on a chalkboard. But waken its neighbors it did, as egrets took flight and pink-backed pelicans left their treetop roosts in awkward flaps of wings.

On this morning, I was joined by a couple of Dutch volunteers, who had been assisting with the marine turtle research project near Gamba town led by Ibonga. Along with Jean Pierre and Martin Ombenentori, our local ornithologist and guide, who had accompanied me to see the rosy bee-eaters the year before, we were traveling up into Loango National Park by way of a motor-powered boat. We were testing out a tourist route to assist in developing safe, interesting trails for emerging ecotourism potential in the region; we were on our way to enjoy a day of hiking through the park and descending back along the beach, where Jean Pierre would pick us up in the afternoon. This was a popular tourist walk called *"la boucle,"* or the loop (literally translated as "the curl").

We had left Setté Cama village early in the morning, heading out into the lagoon and traveling northwest toward the embouchure, or the mouth of the lagoon, where the ocean enters through a narrow break in the sandy Gabonese coastline. Nearing the embouchure, Jean Pierre angled the boat directly north, into what seemed like a river, and into the muddy mangrove waters. Mangroves rose around us on both sides, their fingered roots reaching out, as if they could walk along the muddy river bottom. Kingfishers and parrots cried out in their high-pitched calls from within the dense tangles, and a fish eagle flew by overhead. Palm-nut vultures soared in the skies above, and we kept our eyes peeled for more wildlife.

Occasional breaks in the mangroves showed grassy mud banks, which were announced occasionally by strong sulfur smells, as the sticky mud exuded these gassy odors. From previous trips, I knew that buffalo, antelope, and other creatures frequented these mud banks, so we all kept a close lookout. The river snaked around several bends, and Jean Pierre guided the boat expertly in the deeper channels, away from sunken sand and mud bars. As we rounded one corner, we heard a splash above the muted roar of the engine. A huge ripple pushed out waves from the shore toward the boat. Only one thing could have made such a large splash and ripple.

Jean Pierre cut the engine and the boat glided to a stop in the deepest part of the river. We waited, with breath bated. And then...two rounded shapes, followed by huge rolling eyeballs poked up out of the water. A massive brown-gray head, tinged with pink, emerged, swiveling toward us, and enormous nostrils snorted loudly, blowing water in a spray. An African hippopotamus, a full-grown male, glaring at the trespassers in the boat. Then another set of round ears, followed by a smaller head, emerged, and another. Three in all, watching us, watching them.

Hippos are extremely territorial, nearsighted, and short-tempered. They are formidable on land, where they can run in very fast bursts of speed; and in the water, they are a force to be reckoned with, as numerous travelers, locals, and explorers have recounted stories of hippos tipping over canoes and large boats. But I had not heard of any such stories in the Ndougou Lagoon, although hippo sightings were common, as I knew from my own surprise close encounter with one while bathing in Setté Cama. In any case, they were not to be taken lightly, and as much as we enjoyed seeing them, we still played it safe by staying out in the deeper water.

When a hippo opens his or her mouth, it is easy to see why they are so formidable, with their long, tusklike teeth, powerful muscles, and, frankly, their general enormity. The largest one here opened his mouth in our general direction, as if yawning, but more likely to show off his strength. The smallest hippo disappeared back under the water, capable of holding its breath for minutes at a time. We watched, trying to guess where it would reappear. Less than a minute later, its head crested the surface downstream from us, headed back toward the open lagoon. The other two, including the big male, followed suit, though slowly, and with no apparent fear of the five primates sitting still in the motorboat. We watched for several minutes as they disappeared, then reappeared fifty yards downstream, then repeated this retreat toward more open waters—and, perhaps, better feeding grounds of the grasses away from the mangroves. We watched, thankful that the big male did not suddenly surface under our boat to capsize us, and happy to have witnessed the majesty of these incredible masters of the lagoon.

Pulling the cord to start the outboard motor, Jean Pierre smiled broadly at the two Dutchmen. We sat back and enjoyed the ride as we edged further into the park, closer to our jumping-off point, ready for the next hippo, the next bend in the river; ready for a beautiful day exploring the waters, the forest, and the landscapes of Loango National Park.

Over the next couple of years, we led other tour groups through the lagoon and *La Boucle* trail. Through Ibonga, with technical and financial assistance from the European Union and Bas Huijbregts of WWF, we were able to organize and train villagers to work as boat pilots, park guides, and cultural and tourist liaisons to visitors from Gabon, Europe, the United States, Canada, and other places around the world.

Hippos in the Ndougou Lagoon near Loango National Park

Following Footprints in the Sand

∽

A breeze stirred the fine particles of sand off of the coarse, tanned beach. This wind, traveling from south to north the entire length of the country, brought in downwind odors of briny foam, washed up seaweed and the occasional hint of something mammalian. The ocean currents also followed this south-to-north trajectory, part of the Benguela current system. Sea life—whales, fish, marine turtles—all were swept along their migrations by this current. Some creatures, especially humpback whales and leatherback turtles, have been documented traveling from the shores of South America through the mid-Atlantic to the shores of Gabon.

And this seemingly isolated beach witnessed the waves, the currents, and the migrations of these great creatures. This beach has also witnessed the travels and works of man for centuries. In the last hundred years, the forests reaching down from the lowlands toward the ocean have been logged for certain tree species, including the versatile okoumé, used for plywood, among other things. Rusting metal fragments of timber-loading ships and mechanical loading docks can still be seen in the shallower waters. Further inland, vast onshore oil wells are reaching their final days of large-scale production. And modern fishing boats, mostly illegally fishing off of this portion of the shore, ply their trade of gathering (overexploiting, in most cases) the bounty of the ocean.

As recently as fifty years ago, this beach was also the site of high-end safari hunting. Distinguished figures from French presidents to wealthy businessmen came to hunt the bounties of the forest. And for generations before and since, indigenous communities have lived, hunted, fished, and farmed in this area. Today, many of the past different ethnic groups have moved on, and the current population of predominantly Balumbu people is quite small.

And with all of this oft-unwritten history, animal diversity, and continual south-to-north wind and current, a large portion of this beach-forest ecosystem now forms Loango National Park.

The breeze continued up through mangrove islands and tickled the feathers on Caspian terns, breathing lightly over the swaying palms and brushed past my cheek on its way north. The hot sun quickly removed any coolness the breeze had brought my companions and me. It seemed to bake the briny humidity into our pores as we strolled downwind, eyes scanning the shoreline, the ocean, and the forest above us calmly, yet intently.

The direction of the wind allowed us to come upon animals at the forest edge or even on the beach before they could smell us, offering opportunities to observe forest elephants grazing on the short brush that was constantly battling the encroaching sylvan refuge in which these majestic beings lived. Reddish forest buffalo used the beach as an easy highway and often cooled off in tannin-laden tidal pools. All in all, it was an idyllic place to get close to wildlife. This was the last portion of the *La Boucle* trail, and I was leading a group of friends on an ecotour.

Out in the open waters, we sometimes got really lucky and were able to spot a whale spout, or even a breaching humpback. Closer to shore, dolphins played the waves, and green turtles feasted on submerged seaweeds.

On this day, we continued trekking southward, heads swiveling back and forth like some kind of awkward birds. At occasional points along the shore, we came across large, rocky outcroppings, reaching out into the water like fingers. Some outcroppings were merely remnants of ancient geologic walls, leaving behind small boulders and flat, horizontal slabs; others were flat, fifty-foot-tall walls of black and gray cliff.

After scrambling over one of the smaller remnants, we returned to the sand. The tide was out, but I did not know for how long. Thirty feet along the sand, we spotted a footprint—large, round, roughly a foot in diameter. A young elephant had walked here hours before us, heading north. It struck me as both amazing and normal that this stretch of sand should be shared by humans and elephants, within hours of each other. Amazing because of the idea of these giants coming down to the shore; normal because it was only logical they should use the beach to travel, to cool off in the breeze, to sightsee.

While I pondered this seeming contradiction, another footprint jumped into my line of sight—buffalo. I pointed this out to my group, noting that the footprint was partially washed away and showed the buffalo had passed this way as it headed southward. Then another—a four-pronged, star-shaped, twiggy track of an egret. And another, the whispered scratches of one of the tiny, yellowish-white ghost crabs that ran up and down the shore, hiding in their underground lairs; feeding on washed-up vegetal and animal matter; hiding from the egrets, terns, gulls, and anything else bigger than them.

Four separate prints, all within a foot of each other. One of my companions pointed a little higher up the shore, to a tractor-treadlike pattern, leading up to higher ground; the lower portion must have been washed away by the tide. I explained that the tracks were left by a female leatherback turtle, on her way to lay her precious cargo in the sand.

Crossing this path were the four fingered handprints of a distant cousin of ours—a red-capped mangabey. These monkeys travel in large troops, hooting and calling. Like most primates, mangabeys are opportunistic creatures, traveling in trees, on the ground, searching for food and fleeing predators.[31] These tracks showed one individual following the turtle toward her now-abandoned nest. The monkeys have been observed digging out turtle eggs, catching ghost crabs, and feeding on both.

Leaving the turtle nest and continuing our trek, we spotted another imprinted story. This looked like a heavy log had been dragged by short, sharp-edged little hands, two on each side. The drag mark was low, barely noticeable, but at the right angle, it became the foot-, body-, and tailprints of a large Nile crocodile. These reptiles can grow to eighteen feet long, weigh an average of five hundred pounds, and are extremely dangerous if confronted, especially in the water. It was rare to see one of the bigger specimens in Loango, as many Nile crocs in Gabon had been eradicated by trophy hunters thirty years earlier. However, these tracks indicated a fairly large specimen. Crocodiles sometimes place themselves at the mouths of small streams as they empty into small ocean-fed lagoons, waiting for the tide to bring in or pull out fish and other smaller creatures. Crocs have even been seen in the shallows off the beach, possibly pulled out to sea by the very same tide.

We stepped back to absorb the larger scene, laughing out loud in amazement. Elephant, buffalo, egret, crab, leatherback, mangabey, crocodile. Seven footprints...eight if we included our own tracks, all encompassed in a few square meters! All of these footprints in the sand.

Hippo tracks on the beach in Loango National Park

Later, we crossed hippo tracks and more buffalo prints, as well as the owners of those prints, lying on the stubbly grass that ekes out its existence between the forest and the beach. The story written in those few square meters of sand was impressive, and I am positive it is one that continues every day.

Touring through Papyrus

When my family came to visit me after I had been in Gabon for nearly a year, I wanted them to experience, at least for a short while, what I had been living and writing home about in letters. I organized a day trip from Gamba up through the lagoon into the Rembo Bongo river, and one of my colleagues, Anselme Mounguengui, was our guide and boat pilot. This was the same river I had travelled with Michelle Lee and her Smithsonian research team in search of the perfect research camp to explore the Monts Doudou. My parents and brothers were absorbing the scenery, the smells of the wet forest, the multicolored leaf patterns, the blur of white as an egret flew in front of our boat. I enjoyed watching their faces as much as anything else.

The twisting river, bending back around behind its mouth where it entered the lagoon, swallowed us whole, pulling in our small boat from the larger waters of the Ndougou into its muddy twists and turns. Bushes and raffia palm quickly formed a wall on either side of the slow-moving current, as our motor propelled us upstream. Kingfishers and egrets hid in the shadows of the sharp leaves, sometimes flitting by so quickly that it was difficult to distinguish the species. The day was cloudy; not dark, but gray and quiet.

Our outboard motor was the loudest sound on the river, but it was muted, with its small blade spinning underwater. An occasional unseen stick or bunched-up bundle of leaves would cause the boat to bounce some, but our progress was otherwise smooth. Anselme reminded us all to keep a sharp eye out along the banks of the shrouded river for slanted logs, which act as perfect perches for slender-snouted crocodiles and African dwarf crocodiles. We also kept a lookout for soft-shelled turtles, which are visible in the water by their pointed noses sticking above the surface, until they dive and disappear. These soft-shelled turtles are hunted to make turtle soup and are becoming increasingly rare.

We finally identified a Malachite kingfisher, as it swerved in front of our bow and landed on a small branch on the left side of the river, blue and red flashing by like feathered lightening. And one of my brothers spotted a slender-snouted crocodile in time for the rest of the boat to look over and snap a few photos of its prehistoric scales before it slipped into the water. Anselme pointed out a dark brown bird, sitting still atop a bare branch on the right bank, with a duck-shaped bill and a large, curved, pointed crest, extending backward from its head. It jumped up on long black legs and glided awkwardly out over the river, flapped jerkily, and vanished into the foliage. I identified it as a hamerkop, a name derived from the shape of its head. The hamerkop builds large, domed nests in trees, using grass, reeds, stalks, and mud.[32] The boat continued on, and the bird stayed hidden.

As we puttered along upstream, we chatted quietly, still keeping our eyes peeled for new birds, reptiles, mammals, and trees. Anselme angled the boat to the left, toward what at first looked like a small break in the shore but then turned into an offshoot of the river, a narrow waterway through the bushes. I smiled and hinted to my family that we were about to come into contact with an incredible sight, something I had been secretly waiting to show them all day.

The boat rounded a small bend in the river's offshoot, and there it was...a field of green puffs, like giant dandelions ready to release their seeds into the wind. Some of the tall green and reddish stalks hung over the dark waters, and others stood straight and strong, four feet tall. And at the top of these reed stems, soft, thin feathers of green sprouted like giant jade feather dusters. Anselme and I explained that this was a papyrus swamp—that ancient plant used to create paper in Egyptian times—stretching all around us, rising above the boat. Papyrus is a dominant species in swamps along streams around the Ndougou Lagoon.[33] In some places, it extends for miles, creating waving, marshy fields of green, where forest elephants forage and forge deep paths through the swampy mud and grasses.

I remember the first time I had entered this same papyrus swamp, and the looks on my parents' and brothers' faces were priceless. This was one of the main attractions for me on the Rembo Bongo, and I enjoyed bringing tourists to see it, especially because the river channel offshoot then emptied into one of the nearly hidden interior lakes of the area. This lake, Lac Kivoro, branched out with several arms into the surrounding forest. West African manatees are known to live in these lakes, although we did not see any on that day.[34]

However, as we left the papyrus swamp, and immediately before entering the lake, we did observe some of the most masterful builders of the animal kingdom—weavers. These bright yellow, black-headed weavers, properly called village weavers, are called *tisseran gendarme* in French, or the weaver police, as they raise a ruckus if an intruder threatens their colonies. Weavers make elaborate hanging nests, weighing down the branches and leaves of their host trees, including palms. The entrance to the nest is often made quite small and narrow to keep other birds, such as the cuckoo, from taking it over as their own.

After observing the weaver cacophony for fifteen minutes or so, Anselme piloted the boat out into the open water of the lake, calm on this windless early afternoon. He beached the boat on the muddy shore, and we enjoyed a quick sandwich picnic, then took a brief stroll through the tall, gnarled trees and vines.

Later, once we had reboarded the boat and maneuvered back toward the channel leading from the lake to the river, my mother spotted a wading bird with bright yellow legs and something yellow hanging from its beak, stepping gingerly along a shore backed by dried roots and dead twigs. We edged the boat closer, hoping not to scare the bird away. Its head was light gray in color, with a white crown and brown back. A white shoulder stripe followed along midway into a white wing band, leading into a dark black wing tip. These varied patterns, combined with a white breast, meant that the yellow hanging from its beak was actually a set of fleshy wattles, helping us to identify the bird as a white-headed lapwing. None of us had ever seen this bird before, and it was a fitting end to our short time on the lake.

As we headed back into the main river, Anselme angled the boat downstream, hoping to make good time going with the current. We looked back one last time, thinking of yellow weavers, yellow wattles, and green, fluffy papyrus.

Night Surfers

Nighttime. No moon. The dark was inked into the sky, the air, everything. The coastal wind and the lapping waves were the only evidence of movement—heard, rather than seen. Clouds hung low, further obscuring any chance of seeing more than a few feet in front of our own faces. And yet, I lead two of my fellow Peace Corps volunteers along, stumbling across the sandy beach, south against the wind.

We walked in the hopes of stumbling upon a nesting leatherback sea turtle. On this pitch-black hike, we explored the stretch of beach patrolled by the Ibonga turtle research team. Although I had walked this same beach on other nights with the researchers, with students, with friends, and with tourists, this night was the darkest I had yet experienced.

The beach at night is a fantastic place; the wind seems crisper, the smells sharper, and the stars, when visible, are crystal clear. It can also be an eerie place, where shapes at the edge of sight blur into one another, fuzzy and mysterious; where the wind brings strange sounds to one's ears as one strains to see and hear. Sometimes the wind brings a hint of animal musk, for the beach is also frequented by elephants and buffalo, in addition to nesting sea turtles.

We had arrived at the beach in a taxi from Gamba town, only to find that the sandy road had been washed out by rising lagoon waters. This segment of beach sat back against coastal shrubs and forest, with a sort of river filled by dark red lagoon tidal waters. Mangroves edged out on either side of the river, and a low bridge usually allowed vehicles to cross onto the white sand. However, now the water ran high, and we were forced to walk through the rushing dark waters up to our knees, pushing against the current for about fifty yards to reach the safety of the beach. Luckily, the temperature of the water and the air was its usual balmy self, so we hiked in shorts and T-shirts.

Hours later, as we strolled along through the pitch black, we carefully crossed over washed-up logs, seen only at the last instant before they could trip us. We were hoping to stumble upon the distinctive tracks of the leatherback, leading from the ocean up to a higher point on the beach to dig a nest and lay her eggs. We walked and walked, without any luck.

The wind picked up, bringing with it that sharp odor of musk. By this time, however, we had become used to this smell, without spotting any creatures, so we continued walking. We were equipped with flashlights but, for the most part, refrained from using them, as they might scare off or confuse turtles coming out of the ocean. The flashlights were more for signaling to the researchers if we saw anything and for observing the actual nesting process, once a turtle had begun to lay her eggs.

All of a sudden, out of the corner of my left eye, roughly twenty feet in front of us, a massive shadow rushed from left (the forest) to right (the ocean) and disappeared. I whispered to my friends that we should stop and asked if they had seen anything. My heart was thumping, as the shadow had been huge, larger than a horse and much, much heavier. I strained my tired eyes further, watching for other shadows, listening for any sound and sniffing the wind, as if that would give me some clue as to what had just happened. We waited, scarcely moving for the next five minutes. Nothing moved, at least that we could see or hear. So I called for my friends to follow, predicting that we would see something pretty amazing.

Sure enough, we came upon footprints—huge, deep, evidence of a running beast. These were four-pointed hoofprints of a startled hippo, and they led directly into the surf. This was thrilling, to have witnessed (sort of) one of the rarest phenomena of large land mammals: the surfing hippos of Gabon.[35] These aquatic creatures, found in rivers, lakes, and lagoons, as well as on mud banks and grassy land, have occasionally been seen playing in the surf. And on this dark night, I had just seen one headed into the waves. I shuddered to think what would have happened if we had been in that hippo's path, and nervously glanced out at the barely visible breakers, looking for the shine of two bright, big eyes.

We continued on a short ways until we reached the end of the study area, marked by a large, sunken log, where we turned around and headed back toward the turtle team's research camp. We now walked with the wind, so any large animal in front of us would catch our scent and flee (hopefully) before we reached it. We were all excited about the hippo but still hoping to see a sea turtle.

We had walked the southern half of the study area and were making our way back to the center. Some of the turtle research team had walked the northern half. As had happened to me on previous occasions, as we reapproached our starting point, with roughly five hundred meters left to go, we finally came across those distinctive, tractor-tread tracks of a leatherback. We followed the tracks up onto the higher sand and were presented with an impressive nine-hundred-pound, six-foot-long female leatherback, laying small, white, Ping-Pong ball sized eggs, as her species has done for tens of millions of years.

I remember smiling as my friends watched this awesome spectacle and, looking back to the south, I hoped to again see another hippo shadow rush by, headed out to join the leatherbacks that were not yet ready to come ashore, headed out to surf in the midnight waves.

Leatherback turtle headed back to sea after laying her eggs at Pont Dick Beach near Gamba

Funeral Lament

I've mentioned before that the lagoon at dawn was ethereal. The light slowly spreads across its quiet waters like the beginning of a flame, twisting, rippling, mirroring the sky. The winds and rain, when they came, could work the water into a torrent, waves throwing water back and forth, frothing like some terrifying creature. Those days were memorable, holding tight to the sides of a dugout pirogue or a fiberglass-hulled motor boat, bouncing from wave crest to wave crest, sinking in the troughs and shivering in the drenching deluge. But these quiet morning light shows painted recurring pictures in my mind of the oft-silent beauty of the Ndougou Lagoon.

At a clearly orchestrated moment, the forest sounds would awaken to the light and be carried out across the water to listening ears. Whether in a boat or onshore, these sounds seemed amplified by the brackish waters. Bird calls, sharp and soft, long and staccato; shifting trees creaking against one another when a brisk sea-breeze picks up; children laughing as mothers called for chores to be done; or fishermen setting their nets in their boats to begin the day's work. One could sometimes also catch a hint of an elephant's trumpet, a grunting boar, or a laughing chimpanzee rise out over the water from some hidden section of the surrounding forest.

Early one morning, Jean Pierre and I gathered our packs, jumped into his boat at the lagoon's shore in Gamba town, and pushed off toward the village of Setté Cama. Jean Pierre had invited me to stay at his house in the village with his family for the weekend. The day was only just beginning to break, the mists were lifting, and we were excited to shoot across the glassy water. I was entranced by the hundreds of tree-covered islands that seemed to soar both up into the pale sky and down into the dark water. The only difference to my eyes between the dual-islands was the slightly darker and wavier reflection of the downward-pointing trees, as compared to the soaring trunks silhouetted by the sunrise.

Twenty minutes out of town, we left the close-knit islands and entered a more open portion of the lagoon. The sunlight was just flickering through the forest to the east, bathing us in ever-increasing warmth. Above the sound of the twenty-five horsepower motor, I could make out the call of a hornbill. Wildlife would be stirring in the forest—and in the water, too.

I stretched out to enjoy the lifting of the nighttime veil. To our right (the northeast) were several islands near the shoreline, which hid small fishing camps. Throughout the year, fishermen and their families would set up small camps to get away from the more crowded villages or from Gamba town; there, they would enjoy having a small part of the lagoon and forest to themselves. Many tiny cultivated farms dotted the land around the lagoon, and the fishermen often combined fishing with taking care of their family plantations of manioc, taro, bananas, and other crops.

As we passed by the islands, a sound unlike any I had ever heard, then or since, seemed to well up out of the still water. It reached us like a wall and fell upon our ears with such force that it seemed to cut off our engine. Jean Pierre must have hit the kill switch. The sound welled up again, coming in waves, drowning out every other noise.

We looked toward the islands, trying to determine where this acoustic torrent was coming from. Out of the shadows of a nearby forested isle, a small, thin wooden pirogue emerged, skidding along the water, powered by the halting paddle strokes of an old woman. A wail erupted from this figure, again crashing into our now-hypersensitive ears, spiraling up and out, winding its way around us like a constricting python. She seemed to sing her mourning keen, chanting it rhythmically, washing us in sadness. It echoed, carried across the lagoon, bouncing off the islands, and clung hard to my soul. How could this distant, frail-seeming woman generate such a massive sound, I wondered.

As she paddled behind another islet, we spotted the fishing camp from whence she had come. We started up the motor again, muffled still by the wailing lament emanating from further down the lagoon, and motored over to the camp. Jean Pierre called out respectfully to the camp, asking what had happened, why the woman was in so much pain. Not surprisingly, we learned that the woman was crying for a recently deceased loved one.

Jean Pierre told me that her family would prepare a funeral ceremony and *retrait de deuil* (directly translated as "withdrawal from mourning"), not unlike the ceremony I had witnessed with drumming and raffia-covered beasts in Lambaréné. These ceremonies are critically important to Gabonese families, serving to honor the departed, comfort the living, and bring the general community closer together.

Despite the beauty of the morning, we continued on our path in silent, saddened reflection. The utter sense of loss, of bitter heartbreak, played counterpart to the beauty of the morning; and these competing, blending thoughts linger with me still. Rarely have I been swayed to such deep emotion by sound, to feel the goose bumps on my arms, as happens through the perfect pitch of a professional singer or during a performance by a stellar symphony orchestra. The old woman's lament shook me through and through. I believe her song lifted to the heavens and filtered through the earth, and I hope it provided comfort to her and her departed one.

Judgment and Sorcery

"**B**atu baSetté Cama." Speaking in Yilumbu, the village elder greeted his friends and family, the people of Setté Cama.

Switching to French, he went on, "Today, we are here to decide what to do with this grave situation affecting our village."

He spoke loudly, slowly, looking around at the gathered inhabitants of Setté Cama. With glasses hanging at the end of his nose, he seemed to seek eye contact with everyone present. His red felt hat, rimmed with a black band, lay in front of his large hands, resting on the table.

"You all know why we are here, and now, we've come to make a decision together."

Sitting next to him were several other village elders, including the village chief, also with a hat in front of him, although the chief's hat was dark gray, almost black. This small table, set up with three chairs facing the crowd and two on the ends, sat like a tribunal. The old men were the judges, the arbiters of community disputes. The table was situated inside a metal-roofed, open air *corps de garde*. As in days of old, this structure served not only as a place for ceremonies but also as the center of power for the village. From here, village chiefs dispensed their wisdom and judgment.

Jean Mbouity, *l'Americain*, my friend the net-casting fisherman, sat at one end of the table, acting as an adviser to the other elders. The village secretary, an oft-drunk but affable Ministry of Water and Forests employee, sat at the other.

We lined up our chairs on the edges of the *corps de garde*, facing inward and each other, with the elders' table facing all of us. The villagers, young and old, men and women, were agitated. Sitting next to Jean Pierre, I asked what was happening.

Davy Mbouity 2005

Setté Cama village council hears arguments against alleged sorceress

He explained that for the past year, there were suspicions that someone in the village was casting magical spells to scare the others. This person, whom everyone suspected was one of the old women sitting in the crowd, was transforming herself into various animals and terrorizing the other villagers. As he described this seemingly impossible act, it reminded me of Julien, back in Lambaréné, explaining how some people used their training and skills as traditional healers, or *Ngangas*, to help their communities, whereas others used those same skills to harm others.

I was pulled out of my reflections when the village chief raised his hands to indicate he wished to speak. He spoke in Yilumbu, so Jean Pierre translated for me into French.

"For too long, our peaceful village has been under threat by one of its own. We know who you are, and we are here to order you to stop these shameful actions." He spoke quietly, but everyone waited on his words. He never mentioned the alleged guilty party's name but instead asked the villagers to speak, if they had anything they wanted to say.

At first, everyone sat still, some shuffling their feet in the sand. Then, one of the old women stood up. She glowered at the chief, then at the crowd. "If no one else wants to speak, I'll start. This meeting today should have taken place months ago. There is a *sorcière* [witch] living in our village. And for whatever reason, she is jealous of those of us with children who are working, or of those of us with husbands who are bringing back fish to eat. You all know me, and where I live...." Setté Cama had about ninety residents, so everyone knew everyone else's business.

She continued, "Last month, I was inside my home, getting ready to turn down the kerosene lantern, when I heard a soft scratching at my door. I am old, but I still heard it. I thought maybe one of the children from next door was out late playing, so I went to open the door."

She paused for dramatic effect, letting her eyes go wide.

"And there, looking up at me with evil eyes, was a leopard. But those eyes were not animal eyes...no. They were the eyes of a person, the eyes of that woman there!"

She pointed to another old woman sitting near the end of the line of chairs. The accused shouted that this was a lie, that she was not a sorcerer. But others nodded in agreement with the accuser.

"That leopard, it came to my house too," shouted one of the men sitting near me. "You can still see where it scratched my door, where its claws carved out deep marks."

As others joined in, the accused sat defiantly, glaring at everyone.

One of the younger men, a fisherman, stood up. He said that although he hadn't seen the person masked as a leopard, he had witnessed this same type of sorcery, and during the day. Down by the edge of the lagoon, fishermen were being watched and followed by a hippo that also had human eyes. Every morning, this hippo would pop its head out behind his boat as he prepared to leave for the daily catch. He noted that no real hippo would ever have that sort of cunning or be able to recognize a person and his boat. I remember thinking about the hippo I had encountered during my evening bath further north on the lagoon, thinking that this could just be a curious youngster wanting to play. But I kept out of the dispute.

Another fisherman said that his children had also been spooked by this hippo that wasn't a hippo, and that his family was scared. Drawing support from the crowd, he demanded that the elders put a stop to this dangerous magic and punish the old woman, who stood accused.

I looked to Jean Pierre after he translated this entire dialogue and asked what kind of action the elders could take. He whispered that in similar cases, the elders would order that the villagers shun the accused *sorcière* for a time, until he or she stopped the spells. He said in the past, the villagers would take more extreme measures, but he did not elaborate further.

As the villagers aired their grievances, the children of the village ran around and played as usual, mostly ignoring this courtlike event. Mothers sitting in the crowd cradled their babies. However, all of the adults paid close, serious attention to the elders, to the speakers, and to the accused.

As I watched, as part of the crowd but not part of the discussion, I could not but help feeling sorry for the bitter old woman, who glowered at all of us. She lived alone, in this tiny village, and her peers were accusing her of dark magic, of controlling wild animals to harm others. These animals—the leopards, hippos, elephants, and gorillas—were a fact of life in Setté Cama. They lived all around the village and often went through it, sometimes wreaking havoc on homes and crops or injuring the villagers. And yet, the villagers were convinced that these recent leopard and hippo incidents were not natural.

The village chief and his assistants listened to each complaint, to every shouted argument or tearful testimony, until everyone who wanted to speak had spoken. He then turned to the accused, who was still glowering, and asked if she had anything to say.

She had shrunken in on herself, but raised her head and said "I deny all of these claims. I'm just an old woman and have not done any dark magic, or cast any spells. These accusations are all false, and you know it." She harrumphed a sigh and sat, looking down at her feet.

The chief conferred with his elders, huddling in whispered discussion, like solemn judges deliberating before passing their judgment. And I suppose that is exactly what they were—judges seeking just decisions for the good of the community.

Finally, after making all of us sit on our chairs or benches for long, painful minutes, the village chief called everyone to order, asking even the children to gather round and quiet down.

He cleared his throat.

"We have heard your fears and frustrations. We have listened to the village air its grievances, and to the accused's side of the story. These animal attacks are not normal actions. They show a jealous mind and malicious purpose. And yet, they have not resulted in any injuries, or any real danger to any of you."

Several people in the crowd nodded as he spoke.

Looking at the accused grandmother, the chief said, "Here is our decision. You must stop your spells immediately. You must cease your attempts to scare your friends and family, your neighbors. If you do not, we will be forced to take stricter action, and you do not want that. We do not want that. So from this moment on, you must stop."

The elder who had called the meeting to order took his turn. He spoke to the other villagers, saying "All of you will move on from this. We have ordered her to stop her bad acts. We have decided this matter, so it is ended."

In the crowd, we all shifted uncomfortably in our chairs. For me, I just needed to move to get rid of some soreness from sitting for the last several hours. For others, I imagine they were not fully satisfied with the decision. But no one objected out loud. The elders stood up, declaring the meeting over, and put on their hats. The secretary, who had taken notes throughout the trial, closed his notebook and sauntered off, presumably in search of a drink.

Jean Pierre stood up, nodding his head, and told me that this was a good decision and the only truly just result. I could only marvel at the simple fact that the entire village believed the old woman was transforming herself into wild animals and, even more fantastic, that the entire village had come together as judge, jury, and decision maker. I agreed with Jean Pierre that this was a just decision and watched the old woman, judged guilty by her peers and village chief, enjoined from any further alleged sorcery, saunter away, alone and dejected, back to her home not fifty yards away.

As Jean Pierre and I walked back toward his house, some of the children were already back playing in the lagoon. I kept a watch out for any hippos that weren't hippos and leopards that weren't leopards.

The Masks We Wear

On my walls, wherever I live now, there are faces, wise and mysterious, staring out at me, as if watching over me, reminding me of where I have been and where I would like to go. These faces come in many different shapes and colors, mostly carved in dark wood, sharing some features, but each unique, distinct. And each of these faces, these beautiful masks, represents a specific time and place, a specific culture, or at least the part of the culture that I witnessed.

Masks are what we humans put on for many reasons, to hide or stand out, to change, to become something else. And they have great significance, whether it is simply a Halloween costume, where a child can pretend for an evening to be a pirate or a ghost, or at a masquerade ball, where adults practice the art of transformation. And this transformation really seems to me to be the ultimate triumph of any mask.

In Gabon, masks serve many purposes. They allow a traditional ceremony to take on historic meaning when, for example, a person dons a full regalia of paint and color, raffia leaves, and either an actual wooden painted mask or a painted face. That person is no longer a person but a symbol, a spiritual being, pulled from the forest or the grave, revered, feared, essential. And how can anyone from outside criticize this practice, which exists in all cultures? How can anyone from outside ever really understand the significance of that mask, or that tradition?

In Libreville, there is a large, mazelike artisanal market, full of wonderful objects from paintings to batik tablecloths, little sachets of spices and powders, and the innumerable knockoff music CDs and DVDs. And of course, there were carved statutes of people and animals—and masks. The smell of this market, the pungent aroma of old wood and dried paint and of burning incense, heightens the experience of entering an old-world bazaar, of removing the veil of time and participating in history, at least for a brief moment—just as putting on a mask can recreate history and tradition.

There are wonderful treasures in this bazaar for both tourists and locals, hidden away behind the kitsch and mass-produced items, waiting silently until a shopper asks the merchant the story of a particular object. And that story, whether true or not, is part of the appeal (at least to me) of starting the game of bartering, negotiating the worth of an old hunk of wood. A little knowledge helps in these negotiations, because it places the merchant and potential buyer on more equal footing and helps pierce through some of the more fanciful stories about what is being sold. This knowledge might pertain to the style of object (i.e., knowing whether a given mask is from a region in Gabon or not, or recognizing the type of wood from which a statue of an elephant is carved), or it might pertain to some understanding of the motivations of the seller. For instance, if a merchant has a thick Malian accent, but tries to pass off as a village elder from the interior of Gabon, it helps to recognize the accent and cease that part of the haggling game.

A typical conversation with a wooden mask vendor might go as follows (translated into English):

Vendor: "Ah, my brother, a fine day today. What can I help you with, as you can see that I sell only the finest, most valuable objects of culture?"

Shopper (i.e., me): "You do have some very fine-looking items here on display. I'm really only just looking around, and not sure whether I'll buy anything. I do not have much money anyway."

Vendor: "I understand. And not to worry. For you, I can give you a very special price, something you can surely afford. You must not go back home without something to remind you of Gabon, this wonderful country!"

Shopper: "Well, I do like the looks of that mask there" (pointing to a round-faced mask carved from black wood). "What is the story of that mask?"

Vendor: "Ah, you have excellent taste, my friend. That mask comes from the deep jungle in central Gabon. A relative of mine, now dead many years, carved it from mahogany. It represents good luck and strong spirits, and it is very valuable, as it was used in many an initiation ceremony. I do not always display masks of this kind, for it takes a special person to notice its importance, but I knew right away you would be such a person. I can give you a very good price; so what do you think you can offer?"

Shopper: "Interesting. Where in Gabon is it from, and can I hold it for a moment? I do like the looks of it, and if it is truly a ceremonial piece, I might be interested in discussing prices."

Vendor: "Well, it comes from the village, deep in the jungle. Here it is, feel the quality of the mahogany, see the fine craftsmanship." (For those of you who have never shopped for a mask, a tip for your next encounter with such a merchant: every mask always seems to come from "the village.")

Shopper: "My friend, the mask is indeed very fine, although this wood is definitely not mahogany. It is too soft to be mahogany. And which village does it come from? I have spent some time around Gabon and might have been to the place you are referring to."

Vendor: "Ah, well, perhaps it is not mahogany, but it is rare and exquisite—don't you agree?—and it comes from the interior of Gabon, from the village near Tchibanga."

Shopper (laughing): "My brother, I live near Tchibanga, which is famous for its Bapunu masks. This is no Punu mask. And what's more, you do not sound like you come from Tchibanga, let alone Gabon. Might you be from Bamako (capital of Mali)?"

Vendor: "Ah my friend, you must be African yourself. But this mask is beautiful, no? and it will look very good in your house."

Shopper: "I do like the looks of it, but since your story of the mask seems to be untrue, I think I could only take it off your hands for about five hundred CFA" (Central African Francs, roughly the equivalent of one dollar).

Vendor (waving his hands in exaggerated shock): "My brother, my brother, you are killing me. I have a family to feed and cannot part with this magnificent piece of art for that amount. True, it is not a Punu mask, but it is still well made. I certainly could not part with it for less than ten thousand CFA" (about twenty dollars).

Shopper: "Ah, now that is just too much, far too much. I was not even planning on buying anything today, but I could consider taking it for one thousand CFA" (about two dollars).

And so on. This back and forth, this amazingly ancient game of wrangling over the right price, is part of the experience of coming away with something amazing—not only the actual object, but the thrill and excitement of the negotiation. One lesson I learned early on was that the seller will never part with something unless he is making some profit. Eventually, if the offer is too low, he will lose interest and dismiss you; so I never felt bad about starting with a very low price.

And poking around in this labyrinth of clothes and food and art, I came away with some pieces of culture which, although perhaps not traditionally valuable or even all that authentic, represent so many memories for me. My hand-carved Punu mask, depicting a wise woman painted in whitewash, with round eyes and a small nose with thick, wonderful lips and a traditional high hairpiece, gazing down with the typical diamond scarification pattern on her forehead, formed by nine smaller diamonds, rests proudly on my wall. These patterns, according to vendors and actual Bapunu friends, might represent the nine provinces of Gabon, or even the mythic nine Punu clans who came long ago to Gabon.[36]

Drawing of Punu mask

My other Gabonese mask, which holds court equally proudly on my wall, is a light weight, two-foot-long narrow mask of the Fang people, carved beautifully by hand to show a regal black face and high forehead, with cheek scarification marks and leaflike symbols on the white forehead and chin.

These masks, and others from other countries and cultures, all remind me of the time and place, the story I was given when I acquired the mask (whether I believed it or not), and the beauty of artwork and tradition. They represent transformation as well, an idea so ancient, so powerful, that it persists in every culture today. Mostly, though, they remind me of Gabon, of the time I was transformed into a Gabonese and the friends and family I long to revisit.

Love and Weaving

꧁꧂

Her fingers moved quickly over the sand, pulling together strands of dried leaves over and under and through each other. A pile of thin, tan and pale leaf fragments sat neatly next to her right leg, while dark red fragments were piled next to her left. In front of her lay the beginnings of her work, framed between a rectangle of wooden guide sticks. Over and under, Maman Georgette had a practiced, steady weave. She created wonderful patterns with the red and tan leaves, alternating between long fragments for the length and shorter for the width.

The tall, serrated leaves used to make these weavings come from *pandanus* plants, which grow in a forest of small, treelike shrubs near Setté Cama village. They jut out from an inner trunk, floppy spikes of lime green. Each shrub sprouts dozens of individual leaves, edged with sharp protective hooks along the outside. They looked like gigantic pineapples, minus the actual fruit. The women of Setté Cama cut the leaves to dry for their weaving.

One cloudy morning, I went along with a group of seven or eight women as they paddled a wooden pirogue, maneuvering in among the mangrove roots, singing softly in the midmorning light. They edged up to shore and stepped out into the shallow waters, machetes in hand and dressed in multicolored *pagne* dresses. These women, tough and dignified, marched over to the *pandanus* forest, each picking a different plant, and began to work, cutting away a bunching of leaves from the stems of the miniature trees, setting the leaves aside as they cut more. They would gently, but firmly, hold each tall leaf in its center, to avoid the sharp edges, and, with a machete, cut along the leaf border to remove the spiny serrations.

*Setté Cama grandmother cutting pandanus leaves
to make woven mats*

Once they each had a sufficient pile of cut leaves, they tied them up to make a bundle. After perhaps thirty minutes, the women had each amassed a good-sized bundle, which they carried back to the pirogue on their heads.[37]

Once back in Setté Cama, the women untied their leaf bundles and spread them out to dry. Some were cut while still green to desired lengths and widths before drying. Once the sun had done its work (sometimes a matter of days, sometimes hours), the once green and yellow leaves would turn an almost beige, as the color melted out with the heat. Some of these nearly white, dry leftovers were then placed in plastic buckets full of different materials, such as the red bark of the padouk tree mixed with palm oil and mud, creating a natural dye. Once the leaves had soaked a sufficient amount of time to absorb the dye, they were left to hang from frame posts in the village homes to cure. This process left a deep red ochre color, which took on slightly different hues, depending on the width of the cut leaves and the quantity of dye used.

The women then sized and shaped the dyed and undyed leaf cuttings to their desired length before tying them to four-sided wooden frames to begin their weaving. Each colored strand was carefully woven into the overall frame, with the women practiced in making intricate patterns teaching their daughters and granddaughters the ancient art of hand weaving. This entire process resulted in beautiful woven *nattes*, or mats.

Many of the weaves would be used as ceremonial mats, which were given as gifts during weddings and funerals and used as sleeping mats for traditional healing and initiation rituals. Others were less ceremonial, meaning they did not contain intricate patterns but were simply utilitarian—used as sleeping mats for fishing camps or even in the village huts.

As she wove her *natte*, Maman Georgette's granddaughter, Maïté, practiced with a smaller frame, watching her grandmother's more expert work. The master weaver would help her apprentice, pointing out ways to make the pattern stand out or to make the weave tighter. Maïté smiled as her first pattern emerged, pleased to be gleaning this important traditional craft from her grandmother.

Aristide Kassangoye 2003

Grandmother and granddaughter weaving a ceremonial mat in Setté Cama

In addition to her beautiful mats, Maman Georgette's family was woven into my life in Gabon in another way, at once more subtle and yet much deeper. When I had been in Gabon for nearly two years, I fell in love. I had known Maman Georgette's children since I arrived in Gamba and Setté Cama. Her son, Landry, was roughly my age and became a good friend of mine. He worked for Michelle Lee at the Smithsonian Institution and helped me arrange environmental education lessons for the school children. She also had two daughters with children of their own. And Maman Georgette's youngest child was just a few years younger than I. Her name was Doriane.

Doriane and I had become friends early on in my time in Gabon. She had a fine sense of humor, sarcastic at times, which was rare among my friends there. Yet she was serious, driven to succeed in school, and always helping her siblings with their children. She introduced me to many of the families in Setté Cama, as well as in Gamba. Her nieces and nephews were in the classes I taught with Jean Pierre. Gradually, I realized that our friendship had developed into something much deeper, as if woven together by a skilled weaver.

I courted her, clumsily asking for permission and advice from her brother and her mother, giddy at her returned flirtation at first, then stronger reciprocated feelings. At first, we would walk through Gamba town or Setté Cama village, just talking, laughing, learning about our similarities and differences. During this time, we always had a chaperone—usually one of Doriane's teenage nephews. He would follow us at a distance, often borrowing my bicycle, enjoying himself, but never letting us out of his sight.

Eventually, I underwent what I was told was a traditional ceremony for an outsider to pursue a woman from the village—namely, I had to answer a series of intense questioning from the elders in Setté Cama, including the village chief, with Jean Pierre acting as my interpreter and advocate. I sat through several hours of questions from nearly ten village leaders, asking about my intentions and ability to provide food and shelter.

They started off certain that I was unsuited to a daughter of their village, then gradually, with much support from Jean Pierre, warmed up to the idea. The end result was a happy group of men who gave me their blessings in exchange for many rounds of drinks. Their smiles and pats on the back made me somewhat suspicious that the intense questioning had been more of a staged test, rather than serious doubt about my character. Ultimately, I had to gain approval from Doriane's mother. She was a kind soul, warm and accepting, weaving us together.

Doriane and I lived together for close to a year and a half. We traveled to different parts of Gabon and spent a great deal of time with her mother (and the village elders) in Setté Cama, and she was able to visit my family in Montana over Christmas, where she saw her first snow, escalator, and horses—much as she showed me many firsts in Gabon. Living with Doriane changed my experience in Gabon, where I had lived essentially alone, at a distance, for nearly two years. I would share frustrations, joy, disputes, and life with her. And I felt more a part of the community than ever, helping out with family events, including the tragic event of Doriane's father's funeral. I helped provide fish for this ceremony, as part of the group of men who pulled in a catch using the heavy seine-type nets in the shallow waters of the lagoon. I was in love and becoming part of her extended family.

When it came time for me to return to the United States, after having lived in Gabon for three years, boarding the plane while my friends, and especially Doriane, waved good-bye, was the hardest thing I have ever done. We kept up our relationship for some time despite the distance. However, time and thousands of miles of separation are tough stow-aways in any relationship, and they eventually ushered in the end of ours.

During my time with Doriane, her mother presented me with some of her beautiful woven mats. I still have those mats, and they are among my most precious belongings, as they were woven with *pandanus* leaves, remembrances of love, and memories of Gabon.

Language of Farewell

"**M**boloani," I yelled, trying to project my voice up and out over the boat motor, up on to shore.

"*Ah. Mbolo,*" shouted several village elders, squinting out to where I stood in the fiberglass-hulled, green-and-white boat.

I wondered whether these people were trying to see who had yelled with such a funny accent, or whether I had pulled off the greeting convincingly enough so the elders were merely trying to see who was coming. Waving, I sat down and smiled, pleased with this minimal effort of speaking in the native tongue. Jean Pierre, who had taught me much of my limited vocabulary, laughed from his pilot's seat.

Gabon is a country of more than forty recognized languages, falling into various large family groups, such as Fang (in the north of the country, bordering Cameroon and Equatorial Guinee) and Yipunu (encompassing the

242

southwestern portion of Gabon, including the derivative tongues of the Ndougou Lagoon, such as Yilumbu, Civili, and Yivarma).[38] With local dialects and mixtures of language, for the vast majority of people, including those village elders deep in the forest, French is the unifying mode of expression, stemming back to trade with Europeans in the seventeenth and eighteenth centuries, up through the end of colonial rule in the 1960s.

Language is often taken for granted, overlooked in its significance. It helps define a people, giving them an identity in their own words and in the words of others. It gives expression to ideas and concepts, realities, and exchanges with outside actors. And in a place like Gabon, it allows individual villages to distinguish themselves from their neighbors, near and far, and highlights the perceived and, sometimes, hoped-for differences between family, clan, and ethnic groups.

Hence, the greeting concept may be expressed, depending on where one expresses it, as "*mbolo*" (singular) or "*mboloani*" (for greeting multiple people) in Fang, Yilumbu, and many other tongues, or "*marambuge*" (pronounced "mahr AM buh gah") in Yipunu. Most of the local languages in Gabon fall within the larger Bantu family group of languages, which cover much of Central and East Africa, as well as some languages in West and Southern Africa.

Once this greeting is expressed, the response, as in many other languages, reflects an acknowledgement and a return salutation. In Yipunu, the response to "*marambuge*," could be "*Nine, nan ndejua*" (pronounced "neen nan DEH joo ah"), meaning "Yes, I'm doing fine."

In a place like Gamba, where a microcosm of Gabon and the world has congregated to work in the oil fields or for various other groups, it is easy to pick up a few words in many different languages. Mastering any one dialect, however, was not only challenging but, for me, impossible.

Of any one ethnic group, I spent the most amount of time with the Balumbu of Setté Cama village, where I garnered a smattering of phrases and words—enough to understand when people were talking about *"nzaou"* (elephants), *"nzigou"* (chimpanzees), *"ibonga"* (turtles), *"ufubu"* (hippos), *"niame"* (meat), or the *"ibamba"* (the pale interloper with my face and name). In addition to Jean Pierre's tutelage, Doriane helped me expand my Yilumbu abilities and often acted as a translator for me. She was born in Setté Cama, descended from both Balumbu and Bavili peoples.

I also learned enough to come to understand the true power of naming someone or something. Humans seem to have an inherent need to label things, people, time, places, and concepts. Some of those names are more powerful, more primal than others, especially in the case of people. For instance, a person may have several names on his or her official birth certificate, which would be his or her given name for most functions in daily life. Yet, that name, a construct of the written, colonial infrastructure, was only one identity, and a slightly artificial one at that. In that person's native village, where tradition, culture, and language still thrive, a different name was given to describe and more effectively identify the person. This name might reflect how the individual was born, who his or her ancestors were, or when the person was born.

And knowledge of that name evoked a kind of power, the ability to label the person with his or her "true" character, as identified in the name.

This concept of "true" names was foreign to me, and I have to admit that I still do not fully understand it. But I do understand the power of words, of saying what one means and being understood, of pointing to a place on a map and naming it, of explaining a concept, attempting to assert some form of control. My "true" name is my birth name, and it is out there for people to see and hear. So it could be said that I have given up a certain amount of control over my identity. In Gabon, on the other hand, a given name is like the veneer that is presented to others, like a glimpse through the forest, without actually showing the individual nature of the tree within. A "true" name is kept more closely guarded; and even if known, it is not used often.

Being called by one's "true" name is like a formal outing of one's identity, an attempt to diminish one's power by shedding light on one's nature. Sometimes, on important occasions, such as during traditional marriage, funeral, or other ceremonies, one might wish to use one's "true" name, as a kind of affirmative control over one's own identity, a verbal and spiritual flexing of the power in one's soul. And there are degrees to which uttering a person's "true" name may be acceptable. If the naming comes through as a sign of respect, as opposed to an attempt to diminish or control, it may be acceptable to use that name. Jean Pierre was often affectionately, and respectfully, called *Tonton Nang*, which was short for "Uncle Mounanga," as his "true" name was Mounanga.

And it is always appropriate for a parent to scold an offspring using the child's true name, much the same as my mother would scold me using my full, given name (middle name and all).

Yet, what are these "true" names, these instances of powerful cultural identity? My understanding, gleaned from three years of careful, though not fully objective, observation, is that the language used to describe someone or something can sometimes be summarized with one word. For instance, I was given a Gabonese "true" name by my friends. My name is *Moussounda*. This name, so I was told, signifies at least one of the following ideas: it could mean that I was born with my umbilical cord around my neck, or that my birth was somehow difficult. This signifies a symbolic and literal struggle and triumph in my birth. (According to my mother, the doctors did have to turn me around before I could be born, so my Gabonese namers were quite insightful.) Or, it could mean that I was born before or after a set of twin siblings.

In any event, this one word carries with it emotional and historical baggage, which would immediately be known to whoever used the name when referring to me. And in doing so, that person would know part of my history, part of my core; that is to say, that person would have some power over me with that knowledge.

This naming convention still remains mysterious to me, despite the limited knowledge I was able to ascertain. But I do know this: language, and the words and manner in which it is expressed, make up the bedrock of a person's identity and culture. Language helps situate an individual within the larger social group and society, and shared language—verbal or otherwise—helps bridge gaps and build bridges across cultures.

Jean Pierre and I would not have become such good friends and colleagues if we weren't both curious and respectful of each other's language and culture, and Doriane and I would not have fallen in love without the desire to share and understand.

Language helps to pierce the veil of culture, to glimpse through the forest to see the whole and the individual. *Et quand on commence à comprendre une autre langue, c'est plus facile à comprendre une autre personne, une autre culture, et le monde entier* (which is to say, when we start to understand another language, it becomes easier to understand another person, another culture, and the entire world). And that is the wonderful power of language, which is good, thankful, and strong. The Yilumbu manner encompasses all of these concepts into one word: *Diboti*.

After spending three incredible years in Gabon, I came to realize that in this land of forest, water, and people, the hardest lesson of any language is learning how to say good-bye.

As I gazed back at the village elders I had greeted one last time, still smiling that they had understood my yelled-out *"mboloani,"* one of them raised his weathered hand and shouted, his voice having no problem projecting out over the water, *"Kangwalio."* Farewell.

*Last look over the forest and the Rembo Bongo as
it empties into the Ndougou Lagoon*

PART I

1   Rohland N, Reich D, Mallick S, Meyer M, Green RE, et al., "Genomic DNA Sequences from Mastodon and Woolly Mammoth Reveal Deep Speciation of Forest and Savanna Elephants," *PLoS Biology* 8 no. 12 (2010): 1-10, *available at* http://www.plosbiology.org/article/info%3Adoi%2F10.1371%2Fjournal.pbio.1000564. *See also* Brian Handwerk, "African Elephants Really Two Wildly Different Species?" *National Geographic Daily News* (Dec. 22, 2010), *available at* http://news.nationalgeographic.com/news/2010/12/101222-african-elephants-two-species-new-science/; and Lee R. Berger, "How Do You Miss a Whole Elephant Species," *National Geographic News* (Dec. 17, 2001), *available at* http://news.nationalgeographic.com/news/2001/12/1217_leeelephant.html.

2   For an ongoing study on forest elephant vocalizations, see the Cornell Lab of Ornithology Elephant Listening Project, http://www.birds.cornell.edu/brp/elephant/index.html.

3   *Id.* at http://www.birds.cornell.edu/brp/elephant/sections/dictionary/
infrasound.html. *See also* Katy Payne, *Silent Thunder: In the Presence of
Elephants*, p. 121 (Penguin Books 1998).

4   *See* Greg Jones, "Gabon burns ivory stockpiles," *The Guardian* (June
27, 2012), available at http://www.guardian.co.uk/environment/2012/
jun/27/gabon-burn-ivory; *see also* Christina M. Russo, "How China is
Driving the Grim Rise in Illegal Ivory," *Yale Environment 360*, part of
the Guardian Environment Network (Jan. 23, 2012), *available at* http://
www.guardian.co.uk/environment/2012/jan/23/china-rise-illegal-
ivory. See also "Gabon to destroy its ivory stockpile," *WWF News* (Apr. 5,
2012), available at http://wwf.panda.org/wwf_news/?204137; *see also*
Jean Rovys Dabany, "Poachers Kill 11,000 Gabon Elephants in Under a
Decade," *Reuters* (Feb. 6, 2013), *available at* http://www.reuters.com/
article/2013/02/06/us-gabon-elephants-idUSBRE9150HG20130206.

5   WWF Gamba has an excellent video of traversing the Plaine Ouanga
and the ferry at Boumé Boumé, available at http://www.youtube.com/
watch?v=9eJNR6DS1oo.

6   *See* E. M. Mavioga, et al., "Sweet Little Gabonese Palm Wine: A
Neglected Alcohol (Petit Vin de Palme gabonais doux: un alcool
négligée)," *West African Journal of Medicine*, Vol. 28, No. 5 (2009):
291–294, available at http://www.ajol.info/index.php/wajm/article/
viewFile/55001/43479.

PART II

7   For some additional information on the Niembe rites, see the Sorosoro
website: Niembe ceremony with the Punu, Gabon, http://www.soro-
soro.org/en/niembe-ceremony-with-the-punu-from-gabon.

8   Fevers and sickness were often thought to be caused by these
nocturnal visits. For additional reference to these nocturnal journeys
and night-dream airplane rides, see Redmond O'Hanlon, *No Mercy:*

A Journey to the Heart of the Congo (New York: Alfred A. Knopf, 1997), p. 379.

9 For a brief explanation of the Bwiti ceremony, see Sarah Monaghan, "The Bwiti Ceremony," *Gabon Magazine*, Winter (2006): 41, available at http://www.gabonmagazine.com/swf/GABON6/gabon6.swf.

10 For a brief article on musical traditions throughout Gabon, see Josh Ponte, "Alive with the Sound of Music," *Gabon Magazine*, Winter (2006): 36–43, available at http://www.gabonmagazine.com/swf/GABON6/gabon6.swf.

PART III

11 Although I did not have a conventional oven, I did learn to use a Dutch oven while in Gabon. With an old cast-iron pot, I learned to bake desserts like upside-down pineapple cake and mango tart by placing two old tomato cans inside the pot, or lining the bottom with fine sand, upon which to set a glass pie pan in which the cake would rise to perfection. This, of course, took some trial and error, but cookies, pies, and cakes became easier to master.

12 Maryann Mott, "Elephant Crop Raids Foiled by Chili Peppers, African Project Finds," *National Geographic News* (September 18, 2006), available at http://news.nationalgeographic.com/news/2006/09/060918-elephants-chili.html.

13 See, for example, Interview of Dr. Stuart Firestein, Chair of Columbia University's Department of Biological Sciences, by Andrew Dermont, Director of Booking and Promotion for Big Think, on September 22, 2010, available at http://bigthink.com/ideas/25252.

PART IV

14 For more information on the Cybertracker program, see http://www.cybertracker.org/.

15 Yuji Takenoshita, et al., "Fruit Phenology of the Great Ape Habitat in the Moukalaba-Doudou National Park, Gabon," *African Study Monographs*, Suppl. 39 (April 2008):23–29, available at http://jambo.africa.kyoto-u.ac.jp/kiroku/asm_suppl/abstracts/pdf/ASM_s39/3Takenoshita.pdf.

16 See Chieko Ando, "Habituation and Conservation of Gorillas in Moukalaba-Doudou," *Gorilla Journal* 38 (June 2009), available at http://www.berggorilla.org/index.php?id=722&L=1&tx_ttnews%5Btt_news%5D=310&cHash=43146eb924de9e890160b20135a8d4f1&PHPSESSID=96cc061514075859c4bb8d8ca021d5ce.

17 For more information about hunting pressure on gorillas and chimpanzees in Central Africa, see Hjalmar S. Kuehl, Christian Nzeingui, Stephane Le Duc Yeno, Bas Huijbregts, Christophe Boesch, and Peter D. Walsh, "Discriminating between Village and Commercial Hunting of Apes," *Biological Conservation* 142 (2009): 1500-1506, available at http://www.eva.mpg.de/primat/staff/boesch/pdf/Conservation_hunting_type_Kuehl_09.pdf.

18 For an official Fishery Country Profile of Gabon, see Fishery Country Profile, Food and Agriculture Organization of the United Nations, La République Gabonaise, FID/CP/GAB (December 2007), *available at* ftp://ftp.fao.org/FI/DOCUMENT/fcp/fr/FI_CP_GA.pdf. For a study on the fisheries of the Ndougou Lagoon region, see V. Mamonekene, S. Lavoué, O. S. G. Pauwels, J. H. Mve Beh, J. E. Mackayah, and L. Tchignoumba, "Fish Diversity at Rabi and Gamba, Ogooué-Maritime Province, Gabon," in A. Alonso, M. E. Lee, P. Campbell, O. S. G. Pauwels, and F. Dallmeier, eds., "Gamba, Gabon: Biodiversity of an Equatorial African Rainforest," *Bulletin of the Biological Sciences of Washington*, No. 12 (2006): 285–296.

19 For example, see the *World Angler Magazine* website on the Ogooué-Maritime Region in Gabon: http://www.worldangler.com/ogooue_maritime_region.htm.

20 For more details on this zoning session, please see Mike Chaveas et al., "USDA Forest Service Technical Assistance Mission to Gabon, Support to the Conseil National des Parcs Nationaux (CNPN), Mission Dates: June 16-June 30, 2005," United States Forest Service (2005), available at http://rmportal.net/library/content/usda-forest-service/gabon-usfs-trip-report-support-to-the-conseil-national-des-parcs-nationaux-cnpn-june-2005/view?searchterm=ecotourism.

21 While I was in Gabon (between 2002–2005), the turtle researchers included Armel Diramba, Alain Diyombi, Guy Serge Imogo, Sjef Kolenberg, Martijn Korthorst, Jean Kumba, Aubain Mackosso Mackosso, Jean-Christian Mamfoumbi, Calixte Manzanza, Julie Marmet, Eustache Beodo Moundjim, Anselme Mounguengui, Kassa Ngoma, Adolphe Nzigou, Claude Odzeano, Guy Gael Panzou, and Bas Verhage. A summary of the results of this research can be found in the following report: Bas Verhage and Eustache Beodo Moundjim, "Three Years of Marine Turtle Monitoring in the Gamba Complex of Protected Areas, Gabon, Central Africa 2002-2005," published by WWF, Kudu Program, Biotopic, Ibonga-ACPE, and Protomac (2005), available at http://www.biotopic.org/pdf/3yrs final_Gabon.pdf.

22 *See* National Oceanographic and Atmospheric Administration, National Marine Fisheries Service, Office of Protected Species, Marine Turtles, Olive Ridley Turtle, http://www.nmfs.noaa.gov/pr/species/turtles/oliveridley.htm and National Oceanographic and Atmospheric Administration, National Marine Fisheries Service, Office of Protected

Species, Marine Turtles, Leatherback, http://www.nmfs.noaa.gov/pr/
species/turtles/leatherback.htm.

23 Bas Verhage and Eustache Beodo Moundjim, "Three Years of Marine
Turtle Monitoring in the Gamba Complex of Protected Areas, Gabon,
Central Africa 2002–2005," WWF, Kudu Program, Biotopic, Ibonga-
ACPE, and Protomac (2005): 28, available at http://www.biotopic.org/
pdf/3yrsfinal_Gabon.pdf.

24 *Ibid.*

25 *Ibid.* at 17 and 43.

PART V

26 See for example, Simon Fraser University Website, The Material Culture
of Twins in West Africa, http://www.sfu.ca/archaeology-old/museum/
ndi/.

27 For an account of how twins are viewed in the Pové ethnic group,
see Paulin Kialo, *Les sylvo-anthroponymes pové* (Cahiers Gabonais
de l'anthropologie, 18, 2006) pp. 2115-2136, *available at* http://kialo-
paulin.unblog.fr/2009/03/14/les-sylvo-anthroponymes-pove-cahiers-
gabonais-danthropologie-18-2006-pp-2115-2136/.

28 For additional insight into this naming of twins related to elephants,
an interesting source of information is a master's thesis by Bipikila
Moukani Mambou, titled "Interaction Hommes/Animaux chez les Gisir
Gabon" (master's thesis, Université Omar Bongo, 2008), available at
http://www.memoireonline.com/03/09/2027/m_Interaction-Hommes
Animaux-chez-les-Gisir-Gabon46.html.

29 Written by Jean Pierre Bayet (translation by Jason Gray)

30 *See* Ibonga website, Environmental Education, http://www.ibonga.
org/?__target__=env_edu.

PART VI

31   See for example Catherine Cooke, "The Feeding, Ranging, and Positional Behaviors of *Cercocebus torquatus*, the Red-Capped Mangabey, in Setté Cama Gabon: A Phylogenetic Perspective" (PhD dissertation, The Ohio State University, 2012), pp. 162, 212.

32   Nik Borrow and Ron Demey, *A Guide to the Birds of Western Africa* (Princeton: Princeton University Press, 2001), 347.

33   *See* R.H. Hughes, et al., *A Directory of African Wetlands* (Wetlands International Ramsar, 1992), Chapter 4.5, available at Wetlands International Ramsar, Ramsar Sites Information Services, http://ramsar. wetlands.org/Portals/15/GABON.pdf.

34   For information about manatee research in the Ndougou Lagoon and surrounding area, as well as throughout western Africa, a great resource is the blog of manatee researcher Lucy Keith, www.insearchofmamiwata.blogspot.com. Several of her trips up the Rembo Bongo, including pictures of Anselme Mounguengui, are detailed at http://insearchofmamiwata.blogspot.com/search?updated-max=2008-12-17T06%3A58%3A00-05%3A00&max-results=7.

35   *See* David Quammen, "Saving Africa's Eden," *National Geographic* volume 204, issue 3 (2003): 50-77, available http://ngm.nationalgeographic.com/ngm/0309/feature3/index.html.

36   For more on Punu masks, see The Art of the African Mask Website, Exhibition Catalog, Bayly Art Museum, University of Virginia, Faces of Spirits, http://cti.itc.virginia.edu/~bcr/African_Mask_Faces.html; *see also* African Art, Ethnicity, Punu, http://www.art-africain.fr/ethnicity/punu/africa-black-life-rituals (which includes an explanation of the diamond scarification pattern in reference to nine original Punu clans).

37 Women (and men) in Gabon often carried heavy loads on their heads, from buckets of water and boxes of foods to bundles of firewood or *pandanus* leaves. They would often place a rolled-up cloth or shirt on their heads first, before setting the load on top. The neck strength involved was quite impressive, and they were also able to keep their hands free to carry other items or balance on a sloped walk, as well as leaving the back or front free to carry a child wrapped in a *pagne* sheet.

38 See Paul Achille Mavoungou, "A Trilingual Dictionary Yilumbi-French-English: An Ongoing Project," LEXIKOS 16 (2006): 121–144, available at www.ajol.info/index.php/lex/article/download/51492/40145.

Bibliography

Achebe, Chinua. *Thinks Fall Apart*. New York: Anchor Books, 1994.

Ando, Chieko. "Habituation and Conservation of Gorillas in Moukalaba-Doudou." *Gorilla Journal* 38 (June 2009).

Berger, Lee. "How Do You Miss a Whole Elephant Species?" *National Geographic Daily News* (December 17, 2010).

Borrow, Nik and Ron Demey. *A Guide to the Birds of Western Africa*. Princeton: Princeton University Press, 2001.

Chaveas, Mike, Don Fisher, Chris Iverson, and Julie Luetzelschwab. "USDA Forest Service Technical Assistance Mission to Gabon, Support to the Conseil National des Parcs Nationaux (CNPN), Mission Dates: June 16-June 30, 2005," United States Forest Service (2005).

Cooke, Catherine. "The Feeding, Ranging, and Positional Behaviors of *Cercocebus torquatus*, the Red-Capped Mangabey, in Setté Cama Gabon: A Phylogenetic Perspective." (PhD dissertation, The Ohio State University, 2012).

Dabany, Jean Rovys. "Poachers Kill 11,000 Gabon Elephants in Under a Decade." *Reuters* (February 6, 2013).

Handwerk, Brian. "African Elephants Really Two Wildly Different Species?" *National Geographic Daily News* (December 22, 2010).

Hughes, R.H. *et al. A Directory of African Wetlands*. Wetlands International Ramsar, 1992.

Jones, Greg. "Gabon burns ivory stockpiles." *The Guardian* (June 27, 2012).

Kialo, Paulin. "Les sylvo-anthroponymes pové." *Cahiers Gabonais de l'Anthropologie* 18 (2006): 2115–2136.

Kuehl, Hjalmar S., Christian Nzeingui, Stephane Le Duc Yeno, Bas Huijbregts, Christophe Boesch, and Peter D. Walsh. "Discriminating between Village and Commercial Hunting of Apes." *Biological Conservation* 142 (2009): 1500-1506.

Mamonekene, Victor, Sébastien Lavoué, Olivier S.G. Pauwels, Jean Hervé Mve Beh, Jean-Eric Mackayah, and Landry Tchignoumba. "Fish Diversity at Rabi and Gamba, Ogooué-Maritime Province, Gabon," in A. Alonso, M. E. Lee, P. Campbell, O. S. G. Pauwels, and F. Dallmeier, eds., "Gamba, Gabon: Biodiversity of an Equatorial

African Rainforest," Bulletin of the Biological Sciences of Washington, No. 12 (2006): 285–296.

Mavioga, E. M., J.U. Mullot, C. Frederic, B. Huart, and P. Burnat. "Sweet Little Gabonese Palm Wine: A Neglected Alcohol (Petit Vin de Palme gabonais doux: un alcool négligée)." West African Journal of Medicine, Vol. 28, No. 5 (2009): 291–294.

Mavoungou, Paul Achille. "A Trilingual Dictionary Yilumbi-French-English: An Ongoing Project." LEXIKOS 16 (2006): 121–144.

Monaghan, Sarah. "The Bwiti Ceremony." Gabon Magazine, Winter (2006): 41.

Mott, Maryann. "Elephant Crop Raids Foiled by Chili Peppers, African Project Finds." National Geographic News (September 18, 2006).

Moukani Mambou, Bipilila. "Interaction Hommes/Animaux chez les Gisir Gabon." (Master's thesis, Université Omar Bongo, 2008).

O'Hanlon, Redmond. No Mercy: Journey to the Heart of the Congo. New York: Alfred A. Knopf, 1997.

Payne, Katy. Silent Thunder: In the Presence of Elephants. New York: Penguin Books, 1998.

Ponte, Josh. "Alive with the Sound of Music." Gabon Magazine, Winter (2006): 36–43.

Quammen, David. "Saving Africa's Eden." *National Geographic* volume 204, issue 3 (September 2003): 50-77.

Rohland, Nadin, David Reich, Swapan Mallick, Matthias Meyer, Richard E. Green, Nicholas J. Georgiadis, Alfred L. Roca, and Michael Hofreiter. "Genomic DNA Sequences from Mastodon and Woolly Mammoth Reveal Deep Speciation of Forest and Savanna Elephants." *PLoS Biology* vol. 8, no. 12 (2012): 1-10.

Russo, Christina M. "How China is Driving the Grim Rise in Illegal Ivory." *Yale Environment 360* (part of the Guardian Environment Network) (January 23, 2012).

Takenoshita, Yuji, Chieko Ando, Yuji Iwata, and Juichi Yamagiwa. "Fruit Phenology of the Great Ape Habitat in the Moukalaba-Doudou National Park, Gabon." *African Study Monographs*, Suppl. 39 (April 2008): 23–29.

Verhage, Bas and Eustache Beodo Moundjim. "Three Years of Marine Turtle Monitoring in the Gamba Complex of Protected Areas, Gabon, Central Africa 2002-2005." Report published by WWF, Kudu Program, Biotopic, Ibonga-ACPE, and Protomac (2005).

Ward, Jr., Carlton. *The Edge of Africa*. Irvington, NY: Hylas Publishing, 2003.

WWF News. "Gabon to destroy its ivory stockpiles." *WWF News* (April 5, 2012).

Acknowledgments

I have dedicated this book to my family—my family by birth, my family by bonds of marriage and friendship, and my family by shared experiences. Thanks are due to every member of this extended family for his or her support, love, patience, and trust in me to tell this part of my story.

Of course, a heartfelt "thank you" goes to the Peace Corps, to which I owe so much of my life experience and worldview; and to my fellow volunteers, who served with me in Gabon and those who came before and after. Serving in the Peace Corps is really a life choice unlike any other—to bridge cultural gaps, create links of understanding, and expand the minds and hearts of US and host-country nationals, all the while helping make the world a smaller, brighter place. The world needs more Peace Corps volunteers.

For their help on this book, my wonderful wife, Linda Barrera, listened patiently to my excitement and frustrations, took a critical eye to these memories, and helped ensure I was writing what I wanted to say. My mother, Nora Flaherty-Gray, taught me French and English and offered excellent, expert editorial input throughout this book. My father, Randy Gray, infused me with a conservation ethic and the need to lay out thoughts and arguments in a clear and concise manner. He also reviewed early drafts and spared no detail in helping refine my words.

Many thanks as well to Max Gomberg, another former Peace Corps volunteer—whose stories from Nicaragua greatly deserve to be shared—for his thoughtful edits and understanding of the need to cherish my Peace Corps memories. I would also like to extend a deep thank you to Marian Haley Beil and John Coyne from Peace Corps Writers for taking an interest in my story and guiding me through the publication process.

Most importantly, I am forever grateful to the people I met, lived with, grew with, and shared with in Gabon. The residents of Gamba and Setté Cama, and all of the villages around the Ndougou Lagoon, sustained and inspired me, taught me to laugh and cry, and awakened a sort of storyteller within me. I hope I have done them proud and that these memories do justice to the incredible country and lands in which they live.

I would like to offer particular love, respect, and gratitude to Jean Pierre Bayet and his entire family; Doriane Tchignoumba and her entire family; Bas Huijbregts; Manassé Mba II; Armel Diramba; Julien Endeng Nguema; Michelle Lee; Benjamin MacDonald; Hans Magaya; Julie Marmet; Augustin Mihindou Mbina; Anselme Mounguengui; Joseph Ngowou;

Guy Rostan Nteme Mba; Mamy Sacko; Diabel Sow; Carlton Ward, Jr.; the past, current, and future members of Ibonga; the entire WWF Gamba crew; the Smithsonian team; and all of my students in primary and secondary schools of Gamba. Thanks as well to Erick Guerra for allowing me to use his terrific drawing of a typical bucket bath.

Finally, I would like to acknowledge the place I have tried to describe, with its natural wonders, its wildlife and scenery, its challenges and triumphs, its people. Gabon is a part of me, with flickering remembrances glimpsed in dreams and quiet moments.

List of Species Mentioned

MAMMALS		
English common name	*French name*	*Latin name*
Chimpanzee	Chimpanzé	*Pan troglodytes*
Civet	Civette	*Viverra civetta*
Common dolphin	Dauphin commun	*Delphinus capensis*
Duiker	Céphalophe	*Cephalophe sp.*
Forest buffalo	Buffle de fôret	*Syncerus caffer nanus*
Forest elephant	Eléphant de forêt	*Loxodonta cyclotis*
Genet	Genette	*Genetta tigrina*
Hippopotamus	Hippopotâme	*Hippopotamus amphibious*
Humpback whale	Baleine à bosse	*Megaptera novaeangliae*
Leopard	Léopard ou panthère	*Panthera pardus*
Marsh mongoose	Mangouste des marais	*Atilax paludinosus*
Mustached monkey	Moustac	*Cercopithecus cephus cephus*
Putty-nosed monkey	Pain à cacheter	*Cercopithecus nictitans nictitans*

Red-capped mangabey	Cercocèbe à collier	*Cercocebus torquatus torquatus*
Red River hog	Potamochère	*Potamochoerus porcus*
Waterbuck	Kobe défassa	*Kobus ellipsiprymnus defassa*
West African manatee	Lamantin	*Trichechus senegalensis*
Western lowland gorilla	Gorille	*Gorilla gorilla gorilla*

REPTILES

English common name	French name	Latin name
African rock python	Python	*Python sebae*
Black mamba	Mamba noir	*Dendroaspis polylepis*
Dwarf crocodile	Crocodil nain	*Osteolaemus tetraspis*
Green mamba	Mamba vert	*Dendroaspis viridis*
Green turtle	Tortue verte	*Chelonia mydas*
Hawksbill turtle	Tortue imbriquée	*Eretmochelys imbricate*
Leatherback turtle	Tortue luth	*Dermochelys coriacea*
Loggerhead turtle	Tortue caouanne	*Caretta caretta*
Monitor lizard	Varan	*Varanus niloticus*
Nile crocodile	Crocodile de nil	*Crocodylus niloticus*
Olive ridley turtle	Tortue olivatre	*Lepidochelys olivacea*
Slender-snouted crocodile	Faux gavial	*Crocodylus cataphractus*
Soft-shelled turtle	Tortue à carapace molle	*Trionyx triunguis*
Tropical house gecko	Gecko	*Hemidactylus mabouia*

BIRDS

English common name	French name	Latin name
African darter	Anhinga d'Afrique	*Anhinga rufa*
African fish eagle	Pygargue vocifer	*Haliaeetus vocifer*